MUMs
RECIPES
TWO

Produced for
Malawi Underprivileged Mothers

by
Linda McDonald RGN, RM

Published by **Linda McDonald**
www.mumsrecipes.org

Printed October 2007
ISBN no: 978-0-9551690-1-4
Registered Charity no: SCO37759

Front cover & illustrations drawn by **Sally McDonald**

Designed & printed by **Smart Design & Print Ltd**
www.smartdesignandprint.com

To Susan,
Best
wishes
Linda
McDonald

This book is for Mum and in memory of Gran - the two women who have most influenced my life.

UBUNTU

I AM BECAUSE YOU ARE

African saying

CONTENTS

FOREWORD

I first heard about Bwaila Maternity Hospital in Malawi whilst I was myself recovering after the birth of my eldest son in Edinburgh. Linda McDonald was one of the midwives patiently teaching me how to feed my son in the middle of the night as I sat in my lovely clean bed in the wonderful new Simpson's maternity unit at the Royal Infirmary Hospital not long opened in 2003. Linda spoke of the suffering of all too many pregnant mothers encountering complications in Malawi and her hope of saving the lives of babies and mothers in high risk pregnancies there. Her plan was to raise funds with her own recipe book. Well that first volume raised £100,000 and this second volume is set to do even better.

I have my own experience in losing my first child who was born prematurely and I understand all too well what that means as a mother. I certainly wish my experience on no one else and hope ardently that we can all find ways to prevent future losses for other expectant mothers. That is why I am such a champion of Linda's persistent and uplifting endeavours to bring about a better way of giving birth where it is desperately needed.

Bwaila Hospital was called Bottom Hospital (the one that was absolutely not the Top Hospital you see) and was coping with 12,000 deliveries per year with only two qualified obstetricians on hand. Its inadequate facilities meant insufficient staffing, poor infection control and little access to necessary retroviral and other drugs. A mother died every 6 days. Stillbirths and neonatal deaths were heartbreakingly high. Small wonder, it was referred to as being 'born into a hospital from hell'.

This is all changing. The Tom Hunter Foundation is building and equipping a new high risk hospital building in the area. The original Bottom (now Bwaila) Hospital is being rebuilt and updated by the Irish charity, the Rose Project. And the fabulous MUMs Recipes are helping to improve nurses' working conditions, to keep midwives working in Malawi and to encourage more midwives and doctors to work in Bwaila Hospital. Infection control will improve and so will pregnancy outcomes change for the better. The donations made via the MUMs recipe book will undoubtedly contribute to keeping Bwaila Hospital sustainable for the long term.

Every copy of this new recipe book helps to raise these vital funds and with the Royal Bank of Scotland's sponsorship of print production costs, this means that more of your money gets to the front line in Bwaila. MUMs Recipes is a real success story and I am very proud to be associated with the two recipe books. Every mother and child deserves to have good care and the right medical expertise available in an accessible hospital that will bring every chance of a successful birth. The mothers at Bwaila Maternity Hospital can have that chance with your help. Thank you for buying this special book of recipes.

Sarah Brown

Sarah Brown is the wife of the Prime Minister and is President of UK children's charity PiggyBankKids which support opportunities for vulnerable babies, children and young people.

8

INTRODUCTION

With the success of MUMs Recipes Book One, I have built up a huge network of supportive people who are committed to making a difference to the experience of childbirth in Lilongwe, Malawi. We are already meeting the main challenge of improving maternity services in Bwaila (formally Bottom) Hospital.

Such a lot has happened in the last two years. The picture of the foundation stone, which features on the back cover of this book, is evidence of the new hospital maternity wing that is currently being built. The Hunter/Clinton Foundation is financing the project with the help of the Scottish people through STV and £100,000 of MUMs Recipes money. The building of this new high risk wing, which is situated beside the general hospital, a few miles from Bwaila, has the advantage of sharing facilities and expertise between both units and giving great hope and faith to doctors, midwives and patients.

Meanwhile back in Bwaila Hospital, an Irish charity, The Rose Project (Aids in Africa), whose motto is *"living and dying with dignity"*, is rebuilding the existing hospital. This will eventually deal with half the number of low risk women; the high risk ones will be treated in the new wing. Bwaila will be run by midwives and clinical officers. Using the £15,000 raised from the Music for MUMs concert in April 2007 and the proceeds from this book, MUMs Recipes - in partnership with the Rose Project - intends to make a long term commitment to Bwaila in the following ways:

- by sponsoring an experienced midwife to work alongside midwives in the clinical area in Bwaila.

- by contributing to the building of a Wellness Centre. In the words of the Rose Project's executive summary, "Building a Wellness Centre in Malawi will address one of the core issues in the continuing decline in health care services. By providing a caring environment for over-burdened nurses and other health care workers, more will choose to remain in Malawi and to continue working in the health care centre. The Wellness Centre Programme aims to provide a holistic compliment of services for all health workers and their immediate families. Services include testing, counselling and treatment of HIV and TB; stress management; training opportunities; post exposure prophylaxis and a resource knowledge centre for continuous professional development."

- by contributing towards provision of a Prevention of Mother to Child Transmission (Aids) Programme in Bwaila Hospital.

Working on MUMs Recipes has given me unimagined satisfaction over the past few years. It has been a delight to share my favourite recipes and to receive such positive feedback. The minute book one was finished, I began to gather recipes, both old and new, for a second book. I hope you enjoy reading and cooking these recipes as much as I enjoyed compiling them. But a deeper satisfaction comes from knowing how the proceeds from MUMs Recipes is used. Many people reached into their pockets, or sold the first book on our behalf, because they were assured that all money raised from MUMs Recipes would go to a specific project. You have my assurance that this is still the case with MUMs Recipes Two and that the money you have spent will make a difference to the lives of many in Malawi.

Linda McDonald

SONG OF THE MOTHERS

because we are women
because we are poor
because we are powerless

we have been silent

when our babies are born dead
we have been silent

when a rotten foetus is scraped
from our wombs we have been silent

when we are in pain
and no one comes, silently
we have turned our faces from the world

it is not enough that we are saved

a shining machine has no heart
a cabinet of pharmaceuticals
cannot love

we must fashion a different song

                    *

because I am a woman
I am blessed

because I am poor
I shall be nourished

because I am powerless
those who have power will strive

that I be granted
the human rights of all mothers

to cry with the pain of the world
to grieve with all the bereaved

to rejoice and to hope
with a sustainable hope

at the birth of my beautiful child

Tom Pow

after conversations with Dr. Tarek Meguid,
consultant obstetrician at Bwaila (formerly Bottom) Hospital

ACKNOWLEDGEMENTS

As the African saying at the start of MUMs Recipes Two says, I am because you are. This book, like the first one, is a testament to the sentiments of these words. It would not have been possible without the valuable contributions of the following:

- The Royal Bank of Scotland, which yet again has been very generous with its financial support.

- Woman and Home magazine for allowing its recipes to appear.

- Sue Lawrence, Masterchef winner in 1991, columnist for Scotland on Sunday and author of "A Cook's Tour of Scotland", for two of her fabulous recipes.

- Smart Design and Print, who have taken the book through from production to distribution.

Everyone who enthused about the first book has helped to make this second book possible, but there are a number of people whose special skills have made the journey easier for me in ways too numerous to mention; Sally McDonald, Chris Smith, Tom Pow (www.tompow.co.uk) - and my many friends and family who have shared their recipes and memories with me.

I am grateful to Sarah Brown for giving her precious time to write the foreword and for her continued support of MUMs Recipes.

A special thank you to Lorna Pascall. Her expert eye helps with pernickety details like weights and conversions. Without her encouragement and commitment, I would have found the challenge of a second book much more formidable.

And finally my deepest thanks to my wonderful family - Iain, Katie and Sally - who have been with me all the way - to Malawi and back!

STARTERS

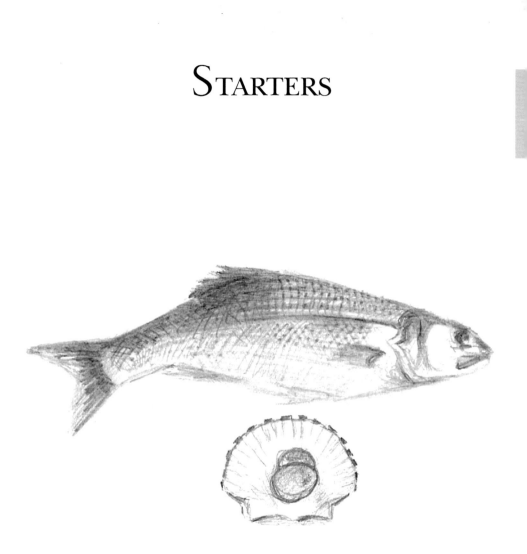

SMOKED SALMON PÂTÉ

(Serves 8-10)

This recipe is easy, makes a generous amount and is very handy to have over a family weekend. It is great as a nibble with oatcakes, or for lunch on toast or simply as a starter with melba toast. I don't have a food processor so it takes a bit of stop starting in the liquidiser to ensure a smooth result.

Ingredients:

400g/14oz cream cheese
300g/10½oz smoked salmon
2 tbsp horseradish sauce
½ lemon, juiced
freshly ground black pepper
1 small bunch chives, chopped

Method:

1. Whiz up all the ingredients, except the chives, in a processor or liquidiser until smooth. Season and chill until needed.
2. Serve the pâté sprinkled with chives.

THAI FISH CAKES

(serves approx 8 depending on the size you shape the mixture)

This recipe comes by kind permission from Café Grande, Edinburgh. I was always on the look out for a lovely Thai fish cake recipe and this is it. You can buy the lime leaves and lemongrass in your local supermarket. This particular recipe can be prepared the night before which is a great plus.

Ingredients:

½ red onion, finely diced
½ white onion, finely diced
2 cloves of garlic, peeled and chopped
pinch of ground coriander
4 lime leaves
1 lemongrass stick
1 red and 1 green pepper, finely chopped
pinch of chilli powder
225g/8oz risotto rice
fresh coriander, finely chopped
juice of 1 lemon and 1 lime
225g/8oz of mixed fish, eg haddock, salmon or tuna
1 fish stock cube, dissolved in 300ml/10fl oz/½ pint boiling water
oil for frying

Method:

1. Heat oil in saucepan and soften onion. Add ground coriander, peppers, garlic, chilli, lime leaves and whole lemongrass stick. Sauté for 5-6 minutes until peppers are soft.
2. Add rice, and approx 300ml/½ pint of fish stock. Simmer gently, stirring, adding more liquid if required, but ensuring mix is fairly dry in consistency.
3. Cook for 12-13 minutes until rice is nearly cooked then add your raw fish mixture, lemon and lime juice, and coriander.

4. Season to taste and cook for 1-2 minutes until fish is cooked through. Remove lemongrass stick.
5. Leave mix to cool, preferably overnight.
6. Shape into small patties and shallow fry for 2-3 minutes until crisp on each side and then finish off cooking in the oven at 200°C, Gas Mark 6 for 10 minutes.
7. Serve hot on a bed of salad, with sweet chilli dipping sauce with fresh lime juice added, and a wedge of lemon.

SPICY PRAWNS

(Adjust quantities as required.)
Whenever I visit my sister Julie and her family in Dumfries we always have these as a nibble when we arrive with a glass of ' bubbly'.

Ingredients:

large king prawns, fresh or frozen defrosted
finely chopped ginger, to taste
chilli powder, to taste
about 1 garlic clove, crushed
juice of 1 lime
black pepper
fresh coriander, chopped
a little olive oil

Method:

1. Stir all ingredients together and leave for a few hours to marinate, or leave covered in the fridge overnight.
2. Heat a little olive oil in a frying pan, add the ingredients and stir on high for a few minutes until crispy and gorgeous.
3. Serve warm with a little extra coriander sprinkled over the top, in one dish or in little dishes, with a mini fork or cocktail sticks. Then again you can always use your fingers!

GILBERT'S SMOKED SALMON MOUSSE

(Serves 6)
Easy peasy! Thanks, Gilbert!

Ingredients:

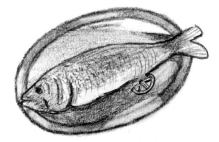

200g/7oz smoked salmon pieces
200ml/7fl oz crème fraîche
1 garlic clove, crushed
1 tbsp olive oil
1 tbsp lemon juice
1/4 tsp paprika
1/4 tsp ground black pepper

See over for Method

Method:

1. Place all ingredients in liquidiser/blender and whiz until smooth.
2. Divide mixture between six ramekins. Cover with cling and chill until required.
3. Serve with melba toast, garnish with a wedge of lemon and a herb of your choice.

Melba Toast

Use 1-2 slices of bread per person.
Put on grill to heat up.
Cut off the crusts and halve diagonally. Toast the bread, split the slices through the middle and toast the uncooked surfaces until slices are crisp and brown. Watch them like a hawk they can burn quickly. Make on the day required.

HAGGIS STUFFED MUSHROOMS

(Serves 4-8, adjust accordingly)
Anything with haggis I love and this is no exception. I have seen variations on the back of haggis packets but this particular one is from Sue Lawrence. Remember you can use vegetarian haggis here also. This is an easy, prepare ahead starter.

Ingredients:

Allow 1 large or 2 smaller, flat, open mushrooms per person, (better to use thin-based mushrooms)
1 garlic clove, crushed
1 regular good quality haggis (remember haggis is already cooked and just needs heated through)
2 tbsp fresh coriander, chopped (see below)
2 tbsp olive oil
1-2 tbsp Parmesan cheese (or any of your favourite cheeses) grated.

Method:

1. Remove the stalks from the mushrooms and place the mushrooms snugly into an ovenproof dish.
2. Mix the crushed garlic, chopped coriander with the haggis. Pile into each mushroom.
3. Drizzle with a little of the olive oil and top with Parmesan, drizzle remaining olive oil over the top.
4. Bake in oven at 200°C, Gas Mark 6 for approximately 25-30 minutes until the mushrooms are soft.
5. Serve with a little salad on the plate and crusty bread if desired.

Note: Chop coriander in an old mug with scissors. This is a useful way to chop parsley, chives, mint, rosemary and thyme.

MELTED CAMEMBERT WITH CRUSTY BREAD

I remember finding this recipe in a magazine years ago and using it often. Nowadays it is very popular in fancy cocktail bars. There are different ways to serve this and I have had great fun experimenting. My good friend Moira, who features a lot in my books, yet again comes up with a lovely alternative - melted Brie and mango chutney recipe which I have included.

Ingredients:

1 Camembert cheese in a wooden box stapled, not stuck with glue
sprinkle of thyme
drizzle of olive oil
crusty bread to serve
warmed cranberry sauce or redcurrant jelly (optional)

Method:

1. Preheat oven to 190°C, Gas Mark 5. Place baking tray in oven to heat up.
2. Peel and discard top lid and wrapper from cheese and place back inside box.
3. Sprinkle with thyme and a little olive oil.
4. Place on baking tray in oven for approximately 20 minutes until soft and runny.
5. Serve immediately on a big plate surrounded by crusty bread and a wide dish of cranberry or redcurrant jelly on the side for dipping. Yummy! Have some paper napkins or kitchen roll at the ready!

MELTED BRIE AND MANGO

Ingredients:

1 wedge of Brie or a whole one for a big party
1 jar mango chutney (if you can get Mrs Geeta's it makes a nice change from Sharwoods)
oatcakes, or crusty bread to serve

Method:

1. Preheat oven to 190°C, Gas Mark 5.
2. Remove rind around the edge of the cheese, this allows the melted cheese to ooze out.
3. Place in centre of quiche or serving dish or something similar that can go into oven. Cover the top with the mango chutney as much or as little as you want and place in the oven.
4. Cook for approximately 20 minutes.
5. Serve with oatcakes, or bread. It is quite handy to have side plates and knives available to make the eating even more enjoyable.

PEA AND HAM SOUP

(Serves 6)

I love the greeny colour of this soup. I buy a gammon steak and chop it small. Serve with homemade

Ingredients:

700g/1lb 9oz frozen peas
55g/2oz butter
1 large onion, chopped
1 pinch sugar
900ml/1½pints ham stock (3 ham stock cubes)
150ml/5fl oz/¼pint double cream
approx 175g/6oz chopped ham
salt and pepper

Method:

1. Melt butter slowly and soften chopped onion for a few minutes.
2. Add peas and toss until well covered in buttery mixture.
3. Now add stock, sugar and 110g/4oz of the chopped ham.
4. Simmer for approximately 20 minutes. Liquidise.
5. Add cream and seasoning to taste. Heat through.
6. Serve in warm bowls with remaining ham sprinkled on top.

TOMATO AND BACON SOUP

(Serves 12)

You can't beat the flavour of greenhouse tomatoes and this recipe Iain makes in the summer when we have a glut of tomatoes, after he has eaten a few on the way to the pot! The tomatoes in the supermarket have very little flavour these days so the bacon helps to make it a tastier soup.

However as an alternative, with some experimenting, Iain has come up with a great tomato soup using tinned tomatoes and to be honest this tastes just as delicious. Freezes well.

Ingredients:

55g/2oz butter
2 medium size onions, chopped
3 x 400g Italian plum tomatoes or 900g/2lbs fresh ripe tomatoes, skinned in boiling water
200g/7oz cheap cooking bacon, cut up with scissors
½tube tomato purée
2 large potatoes, peeled and quartered
1750ml/3 pints vegetable stock using 4 vegetable cubes
1 heaped tbsp sugar
salt and pepper

Method:

1. Boil potatoes until cooked.
2. In a separate large saucepan melt butter, soften onions and bacon for a few minutes.
3. Add all remaining ingredients including the cooked potatoes and simmer for 30 minutes.
4. Liquidise and reheat.
5. Serve in warm bowls with crusty bread.

BROCCOLI CREAM CHEESE SOUP

(Serves 4-6)

Absolutely delicious! This is an unusual soup, great for a dinner party. The pinhead oatmeal, which is used to give the soup its consistency, can be bought in your local supermarket and kept in the cupboard to use at a later date for homemade oatcakes. (See recipe in baking section) Serve with homemade croutons, see below.

Ingredients:

225g/8 oz head of broccoli
40g/1½ oz butter
2 whites of leeks, chopped
1 medium onion, chopped
175g/6oz Philadelphia cheese
2 tbsp fine oatmeal
600ml/20fl oz/1 pint milk
600ml/20fl oz/1 pint vegetable stock
salt and pepper

Method:

1. Trim broccoli into 5mm / ¼ inch florets, chop the stalks into small pieces and set to one side.
2. Melt butter and add leeks, onion and broccoli stalks.
3. Stir, cover and simmer for 10 minutes.
4. Stir in oatmeal. Add milk, a little at a time, stirring well after each addition.
5. Add vegetable stock, salt and pepper then simmer for 10 minutes.
6. Leave to cool. Microwave broccoli florets for 4 minutes in a little water.
7. Pour soup and soft cheese into food processor or liquidiser and blend until smooth.
8. Return to pan, add steamed broccoli florets and reheat gently.

Croutons

I always make my own - very easy, cheaper and much nicer!

Ingredients:

110g/4oz white bread cut into small cubes
2 tbsp olive oil

Method:

1. Preheat the oven to 180°C, Gas Mark 4.
2. Toss bread and oil together in a bowl until evenly coated.
3. Spread onto baking tray and cook for 10-15 minutes on a high shelf, until crisp and golden.
4. Cool and serve or keep airtight for a few days until required.

IAIN'S SWEETCORN SOUP

(Serves 6-8)

This is for all sweetcorn lovers of which my husband Iain is one. This recipe Iain heard on a TV programme and made up a similar version based on what he could remember. The sweetcorn can be used straight from the freezer or defrosted. Frozen sweetcorn is very cheap compared to tinned, so this is a very economical soup to make and it goes a long way. It also freezes well.

Ingredients:

55g/2oz butter
2 onions, chopped
1.1kg/2½lbs frozen sweetcorn
½ level tsp turmeric (this gives the lovely yellowy colour)
1750ml/3 pints vegetable stock (4 cubes)

Method:

1. Melt butter and sauté onions until soft but not coloured.
2. Add ¾ of the bag of sweetcorn to onions leaving remainder to add later.
3. Ensure sweetcorn is tossed thoroughly in onion mixture before adding stock.
4. Bring to simmering point, add turmeric and place a lid on top.
5. Simmer for 30 minutes.
6. Liquidise and strain to remove rough kernel.
7. Place back in pan to reheat, and add remainder of sweetcorn. Heat slowly to make sure all the extra corn has softened.
8. Serve in hot bowls.

CELERY SOUP

(Serves 6-8)

This recipe is one of my Mum's favourites, she, like me, has got lots of recipes on bits of paper tucked in books. It is delicious and freezes well.

Ingredients:

1 head of celery, chopped
1 big potato, chopped in chunks
2 medium onions, chopped
1200ml/2 pints chicken stock (4 cubes)
55g/2oz butter
300ml/10fl oz/ ½pint milk or cream

Method:

1. Melt butter and sauté onions, celery, and potato for 15 minutes.
2. Add 2 pints of stock and simmer for 20 minutes.
3. Liquidise and return to pan adding the milk or cream.
4. Heat through and season to taste.
5. Serve in hot bowls.

PARTY CANAPES

(Adjust quantities as required)

I have made these over and over instead of a formal starter. They are easy, and can be prepared ahead. No real recipe, just put together.

Mini Bruschetta

Ingredients:

1 thin French stick
olive oil
garlic cloves to taste, crushed

Toppings:

sundried tomato paste
mozzarella cheese, sliced small
fresh basil, torn into small pieces
2 tomatoes, skinned and chopped small. (To skin tomatoes, cover with boiling water, leave until skin splits which should only take a few minutes.)

Method:

1. Cut French stick into about 1cm/ ½inch thickness.
2. Place oil and crushed garlic on a plate and dip pieces of bread on both sides to absorb some of the oil. Place on baking tray. You may need more oil and garlic as you go along as the bread is quite absorbent.
3. Bake in hot oven 190°C, Gas Mark 5 for about 10- 15 minutes, turning the bread half way.
4. When the bread turns a pale golden colour remove from oven and cool on a wire tray.
5. Store in a tin for up to four days.

To assemble:
No more than 40 minutes before your guests arrive, spread a little of the tomato paste on each bruschetta, followed by mozzarella and a teaspoon of chopped tomato, finishing with a piece of basil.
These can be served warm, just omit the basil until the end.

Mini Toasts

(for 24 bites, 12 of each variety)
Prepared on the day.

Ingredients:

6 slices of bread
1 packet chicken goujons
cranberry sauce or garlic mayonnaise
1 packet fish goujons
tartare sauce
shredded lettuce
cocktail sticks

Method:

1. Toast bread and cut out with small cutter 4 rounds. Cool on baking tray. This can be done earlier on in the day.

See over for Method

2. Cook chicken and fish goujons according to instructions on packet and cut each strip into 4 or 5 bites according to size.
3. When you are ready to serve, no more than 30 minutes before, assemble the bites.
4. Place a little shredded lettuce on the toast and, then for the 12 chicken bites place a teaspoon of cranberry sauce or mayonnaise on the lettuce followed by the chicken secured by cocktail stick.
5. As above for the fish goujons but use tartare sauce in place of mayonnaise.
6. Serve immediately.

HOT ARTICHOKE AND FETA DIP

(Serves 8)
This was my first experience of artichokes. My sister Nikki brought the recipe back from Denver. The dish tastes wonderful and your guests will definitely wonder what is in it.

Ingredients:

200g/7oz Philadelphia cream cheese (Light)
390g tin artichoke hearts, drained and chopped
55g/2oz Parmesan shavings
2 cloves garlic, minced
1 red pepper, chopped
150g pkt feta cheese and olives, drained, cheese crumbled and olives sliced
tortilla chips to serve

Method:

1. Preheat oven to 180°C, Gas Mark 4.
2. Mix cream cheese, artichokes, Parmesan and garlic till well blended.
3. Spread in an ovenproof serving dish, top with peppers and feta cheese.
4. Bake for 20 minutes, top with olives.
5. Serve with tortilla chips

CRUNCHY SAUSAGE BITES

(Serves 24)
These are great with drinks or, as I made them recently, part of an afternoon tea.

Ingredients:

1 packet skinless sausages
1 piece of sliced white bread per sausage
grain mustard
butter
tomato ketchup to serve

Method:

1. Cut off crusts from bread and roll bread with a rolling pin until quite thin.
2. Lightly spread with mustard and place one sausage at one end of the bread.
3. Roll up sausage tightly with the bread and make sure the bread sticks down at the end. You can use a little butter to do this if needed.
4. Now spread a little butter over the top of the roll and cut in half.
5. Place on baking tray and place on a high shelf in a preheated oven 200°C, Gas Mark 6 for about 20-25 minutes until brown and crisp.
6. Serve hot with tomato ketchup in a small dish on the side.

Lunches & Light Suppers

JULIE'S SEAFOOD PASTA

(Serves 4-6)
My sister Julie frequently uses this recipe when needing a quick supper dish for entertaining friends. Serve with warm crusty ciabatta and a leafy herb salad.

Ingredients

1 finely chopped onion
1 or 2 packets king prawns
4 salmon fillets, cut into smallish pieces
4 slices smoked salmon cut into strips or the smoked salmon flakes (these are often cheaper)
1 tsp curry powder
1 tsp flour
a glass of fresh orange juice
1 orange, zest and juice
a large splash of double cream or crème fraîche
linguine pasta- read instructions on packet to measure correct amounts
black pepper
fresh basil leaves, torn

Method:

1. Start by putting the pasta into boiling water. Cooking the sauce takes about the same time as it takes to cook the pasta.
2. Fry onion gently in olive oil in a medium sized pan adding the curry powder and flour and stirring for a few minutes.
3. Add all the orange juice and zest and reduce (simmering resulting in reduction) for a few minutes until syrupy.
4. Add the raw chopped salmon fillet and stir to cook through, then add the prawns.
5. Add the double cream or crème fraîche with the smoked salmon and a good grinding of black pepper.
6. Stir together gently until all combined.
7. When the pasta is cooked mix in the sauce or pour over the top of the pasta.
8. Serve with the fresh basil over the top and with the suggested accompaniments mentioned above.

EGGS CROQUOTTE

(Serves 4)
This easy lunch time snack was my Dad's favourite when we were children. I still love it.

Ingredients:

4 eggs
25g/1oz butter
25g/1oz plain flour
300ml/ ½ pint milk
25g/1oz Cheddar cheese, grated
1 garlic clove
a little extra grated cheese
ramekin dishes to serve

Method:
1. Rub inside of ramekins with garlic clove or crushed garlic.
2. To make the sauce, put the butter, flour and milk into a small pan and whisk over a gentle heat until thickened, about 5 minutes. Season and stir in 25g/1oz cheese.
3. Divide sauce between ramekins. Fill ³/₄ of the way up to allow room for the egg.
4. Crack an egg over the top and scatter a little grated cheese over the egg.
5. Place in a hot oven 200°C, Gas Mark 5 for about 15-20 minutes.
6. Serve on salad size plates with fingers of toasts around the side.

IRENE'S EASY PASTA
(Serves 4)

I had this at Irene's house on one of our many girls' nights with our friend Babs. I asked Irene for the recipe and these are her words.

Ingredients:
500g fusilli pasta
1 small onion, sliced
1 tbsp olive oil
3 chorizo sausages
125ml/4fl oz white wine (or sherry if you've drunk all the wine)
230ml/8fl oz double cream
approx 1 tbsp Parmesan cheese, grated
salt and black pepper

Method:
1. Heat oil in pan and soften onion without colouring.
2. Remove the skin from the sausages and cut the meat into small pieces.
3. Put the meat in the pan with the onions and add the wine.
4. After 10 minutes add the cream and simmer gently uncovered for a further 10 minutes.
5. Remove from heat and add salt and pepper to taste.
6. In another large pan cook the pasta following instructions being careful not to over cook. Drain well. Toss in the grated Parmesan cheese and the sauce, heat through.
7. Serve immediately in a warmed serving dish.

Note: Marks and Spencers sell a pack of six chorizo sausages so will do two meals (they freeze). I find the sauce can be made in the morning- off I go to work- the pasta is then cooked at night, reheat the sauce gently and mix in the cooked pasta. It's a doddle!

BEANY WEDGES
(Serves 4)

Had this recipe for years. A quick and easy tea for all the family. Serve with sausages.

Ingredients:
2 large or 3 medium baking potatoes, cut into wedges
1 tbsp oil
1 x 420g can of baked beans
1 x 250g jar pizza sauce
1-2 tbsp brown sauce
3 tbsp fresh chopped parsley
110g/4oz Cheddar cheese, grated

See over for Method

Method:

1. Preheat oven to 200°C, Gas Mark 6.
2. Toss potato wedges with oil and ½ tsp salt in a shallow ovenproof dish. Bake for 30 minutes, turning once, until golden and crisp.
3. Mix together the baked beans, pizza sauce and brown sauce. Season with freshly ground black pepper. Stir in the parsley.
4. Remove the wedges from the oven and pour the beans and sauce mixture over the top. Sprinkle over the grated cheese and return to the oven for a further 20 minutes until the cheese is golden and the beans are bubbling.

STUFFED CRUST PIZZA

(Serves 4)
Homemade pizza and fun as well!

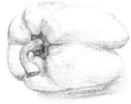

Ingredients:

2 x 148g packets pizza-base mix
85g/3oz grated mozzarella cheese
2 spring onions, finely chopped
110g/4oz mushrooms, wiped and sliced
1 tbsp olive oil
4 tbsp sundried tomato paste
½green and ½yellow pepper, deseeded and thinly sliced into rings
55g/2oz pepperoni sausage, thinly sliced
110g/4oz mozzarella cheese, sliced
few fresh basil sprigs to garnish

Method:

1. Make up the pizza-base mixes together according to the packet instructions. Turn out onto a lightly floured surface then knead for 5 minutes to form a smooth dough. Roll out to a 33cm/13 inch circle and then transfer to a greased and floured baking sheet.
2. Mix together the grated mozzarella cheese and the spring onions and season with salt and freshly ground black pepper. Spread the cheese mixture in a thin ring on the pizza base, about 2.5cm/1 inch in from the edge. Lightly brush the edge with water.
3. Fold in the edge of the pizza base to completely enclose the cheese filling. Press down well to seal. Cover loosely with cling film and leave in a warm place for 40 minutes until the dough has risen. Fry the mushrooms in the oil for 3-4 minutes until browned.
4. Spread tomato paste over pizza, then top with peppers, pepperoni sausage and mushrooms. Bake at 220°C, Gas Mark 7 for 10 minutes, then top with sliced mozzarella cheese and bake for a further 5 minutes. Serve garnished with fresh basil leaves.

CREAMY TAGLIATELLE

(Serves 4)
An easy tea especially for children. Remember to freeze the egg whites for pavlovas and meringues.

Ingredients:

225g/8oz tagliatelle
55g/2oz softened butter

2 egg yolks
110g/4oz grated Cheddar cheese
4 tbsp double cream
salt and pepper

Method:

1. Boil pasta in salted water, drain and return to pan.
2. Beat butter, yolks, cheese, cream and salt and pepper.
3. Mix into pasta and heat through.

TOMATO, BRIE AND BASIL TARTLET

(Serves 4)

This is a made up dish with few ingredients. It looks great and tastes wonderful when put together and cooked. Serve as a light supper dish or for a girls' lunch with a green salad and a glass of chilled wine. Delicious!

Ingredients:

1 sheet of ready rolled puff pastry
1 x 190g jar sundried tomato paste
3 tomatoes
1 wedge of Brie or Camembert, sliced
1 yellow or red pepper, roasted
fresh basil leaves, each torn into 2 or 3 pieces (keep some back for decoration)
red onion, sliced (optional)
pine nuts (optional)
a little milk

Method:

1. Preheat oven to 200°C, Gas Mark 6.
2. Firstly skin tomatoes by covering them in boiling water and leaving them for a minute. Prick skin with a knife, drain off water and remove skin. Slice and leave to one side.
3. Roast pepper by placing under grill and turning it to get an even blackened skin. Place in a polythene bag and allow to cool and shrink. Now remove seeds, stem and skin, slice thinly. This can be done a few hours before needed. Now you are ready to assemble the tartlets.
4. Roll out the pastry and cut into four rectangles. Place on a greased baking tray.
5. Spread approx. 2 tsp of sundried tomato paste on each pastry leaving 2.5cm/1 inch around the edge, clear of paste. Divide the tomatoes, onion (if using) and roasted pepper equally between each pastry. Add the Brie and basil leaves, finishing off with the pine nuts.
6. Wipe a little milk around the edges where the pastry will rise to help colour while cooking.
7. Cook in a hot oven for about 15 minutes. Keep an eye on them because they may take less time and they can burn easily. The sides should have risen and be light brown in colour with the cheese melted.
8. Serve immediately.

SMOKEY CHICKEN PIZZA

(Serves 6)

I love this recipe, because it has all my favourite ingredients in it; Applewood smoked cheese, pine nuts, coriander and chicken which of course can be omitted for a vegetarian version. For an even quicker version put the topping on any naan bread, as Audrey suggested. Suitable for freezing.

Ingredients:

For the base:
280g pkt pizza mix
1 tsp ground coriander
½ tbsp olive oil, plus extra for brushing

For the topping:
200g/7oz can chopped tomatoes
4 tbsp smokey barbecue sauce
2 large skinless chicken breast fillets, diced
3 tbsp chopped fresh coriander, plus extra for sprinkling
½ small red onion, thinly sliced
175g/6oz Applewood smoked cheddar, grated
1 tbsp pine nuts

Method:

1. Preheat the oven to 220°C, Gas Mark 7.
2. Tip the pizza mix into a bowl, add the ground coriander and mix in the directed amount of water on the packet (around 200ml/⅓ pt) and the oil.
3. Knead the dough on a lightly floured surface until smooth, then shape into a 30cm x 23cm /12 x 9 inch oblong and place on a non-stick baking tray. Brush lightly with oil, then cover with clingfilm and set aside in a warm place to rise.
4. To make the topping, drain the juice from the tomatoes, then mix them with the barbecue sauce, chicken and coriander. Spread on to the pizza base, scatter with the onion, cheese and pine nuts and bake for 15 to 20 minutes until risen and golden and the chicken is cooked.
5. Serve scattered with the extra coriander.

SMOKED HADDOCK TART

(Serves 8)

This is a great dish for a summer buffet. You can freeze or make this tart the day before, then just flash the thawed tart in the oven for about 5 minutes.

Ingredients:

450g/1lb rich shortcrust pastry
200g/7oz baby leeks, thinly sliced
25g/1oz butter
400g/14oz smoked haddock
pinch saffron strands
5 egg yolks
350g/12fl oz double cream
110g/4oz Gruyère cheese, grated

Method:

1. Preheat the oven to 180°C, Gas Mark 4. Grease a 27cm/10 ½ inch loose bottomed fluted tart tin. Roll out pastry and line the tin, leaving the pastry overhanging. Chill for 20 minutes. Put on a baking sheet, cover with foil and fill with baking beans and bake for 15 minutes, then remove beans and bake for 5 minutes. Trim the excess pastry with a knife. Reduce the oven to 160°C, Gas Mark 2 ½. Cook the leeks in the butter - you don't want them to colour.

2. Put the haddock into a large sauté pan, cover with water, add the saffron, bring to the boil and simmer for 5 minutes. Remove the fish and leave to cool. Break into chunky flakes, discarding the skin and bones. Whisk together the yolks and cream with half the Gruyère. Place on a baking sheet and bake for 30 minutes. Leave to cool slightly then serve.

RED ONION TART

(Serves 12)

Red onions have a lovely sweet flavour. This is an easy dish and looks great served with a green salad.

Ingredients:

55g/2oz butter
2 tbsp olive oil
1.1kg/2½lb red onions, thinly sliced into rounds
1 tbsp light muscovado sugar
175ml/6fl oz white wine
4tsp white vinegar
1tbsp chopped fresh thyme, plus extra to garnish
450g/1lb puff pastry
plain flour to dust

Method:

1. Preheat oven to 220°C, Gas Mark 7. Lightly grease two 23cm/9 inch non-stick sandwich tins with a little of the butter and set aside.

2. Melt the remaining butter with the oil in a large, non-stick frying pan. Add the onions and sugar. Fry for 10-15minutes or until soft and golden.

3. Add wine, vinegar and thyme. Bring to the boil, bubble until the liquid has evaporated. Season, then divide onion mixture between tins. Leave to cool.

4. Halve the pastry. Roll out each piece thinly on a lightly floured surface into a rough round shape that's just larger than the sandwich tin. Put the pastry over the onion mixture and tuck in the edges. Prick the dough all over with a fork.

5. Cook the tarts for 15-20 minutes or until the pastry is risen and golden. Take out of the oven and put a large warm plate over the pastry. Turn over and shake, holding the tin in place. Remove tin. Cut into wedges and serve scattered with thyme.

Linda McDonald's amazing efforts to support the people of Malawi are mirrored across Scotland, from school links to building much needed hospitals. By buying this book, you too are now part of the national effort by the people of Scotland and beyond to contribute to the development of Malawi. You are helping to change and save lives.

Thank you.

Rt Hon Jack McConnell MSP
First Minister of Scotland 2001 - 07

Main Courses

STICKY RIBS

(Serves 4)

A lovely, tasty Saturday treat. I recommend you serve this with the coleslaw, homemade potato wedges (placed up and down in individual ramekins) and onion rings. Don't forget a napkin and separate fingerbowl for everyone, containing warm water and a good slice of lemon or lime, to clean those sticky fingers!

Ingredients:

900g/2lb lean pork spare ribs
110g/4oz Hoisin sauce
2 tbsp mild clear honey
2 tsp English mustard
3 tsp white wine or cider vinegar
4 tbsp tomato ketchup
2 garlic cloves, crushed
4 tbsp fresh apple or orange juice

Method:

1. Preheat the oven to 180°C, Gas Mark 4.
2. Line a large roasting tin with foil, spread over ribs.
3. Whisk together remaining ingredients for the sauce and spoon over the ribs. Cover with foil. At this stage you can leave for a few hours if you prefer.
4. When you are ready to cook, place tin in the oven, middle shelf for 20 minutes then uncover, turn ribs over and cook for a further 40-50 minutes, basting with the liquid occasionally until most of the liquid is gone.
5. Place the ribs in a wide serving dish and place on the table with above accompaniments.

PORK FILLET WITH CHOPPED HAZELNUTS AND TWO SAUCES SERVED ON A BED OF MIXED PEPPERS

(Serves 6)

This is dinner party material and delicious, but fairly easy. The sauces can be made ahead as can the peppers.

Ingredients:

1kg/2lb 4oz pork fillet (it comes as a roll, often vacuum packed)
150g/5 ½oz chopped hazelnuts
1 heaped tsp chopped rosemary
1 egg, beaten
1 rounded tbsp plain flour
55g/2oz butter
1 tbsp oil
salt and pepper

Method:

1. Preheat the oven with baking tray in, 200°C, Gas Mark 6.
2. Mix rosemary with egg and leave for a couple of hours on a large flat plate, to improve flavour.
3. Trim ends of fillet and season flour.

4. Roll fillet in flour, then dip in egg, then roll in hazelnuts. It is easier to do all this on dinner plates. This can be prepared ahead and left in the fridge
5. Cut into 3cm/1¼ inch slices.
6. Melt butter with oil in frying pan and brown pork slices, transferring them to the baking tray in the oven.
7. Cook for 7-10 minutes in the oven.

Ingredients for mustard and honey sauce:

250ml/8fl oz double cream
1 shallot
2 heaped dessertspoons wholegrain mustard
1½ tsp honey
1½ tsp soya sauce

Method:

Put all ingredients in a pan, bring to boil and simmer for 3-4 minutes.

Instructions for apple sauce:

Either buy a jar from a supermarket or make your own. Buy 2 cooking apples, peel, slice and cook in a pot with a little water and sugar until pulp. Cool and serve with a little rosemary to decorate.

Instructions for mixed peppers:

Buy 2 each of red, green and yellow peppers, slice and stir fry in a little olive oil until soft. Make a small mound of peppers in the middle of each warm plate. Divide the medallions between each plate, placing them on the peppers. Serve the sauces on each side of the pork or separately on the table.

BAKED HAM

Served with glazed carrots (recipe book 1), celery sauce, creamed turnip, and roast potatoes (recipes further on)
I was asked by my family to include this main meal and all the trimmings. Well worth the effort and great for a large number of people for Sunday lunch, special occasion or cold as part of a buffet.

Ingredients:

1 large ham, so that it fits inside a big pot comfortably
about 24 cloves
3 heaped tbsp prepared English mustard
3 heaped tbsp demerara sugar

Method:

1. Wash ham in cold water.
2. Place ham inside pot and cover with cold water and bring to the boil. Simmer for about 2-3 hours. I turn the ham over very carefully half way. You might not need to do this, but make sure the water covers all the ham. Keep topping the pan up with boiling water as the water does evaporate. Test with a fork and make sure juices are clear. I then switch off the cooker and allow the ham to sit for a while in the water.

See over for Method

3. Drain off the water and, lifting the ham very carefully using two strong forks, place ham in a large roasting tin. Now the fun begins!
4. The ham will have a thick skin on it, so with a sharp knife remove it, carefully leaving a good layer of fat underneath. This is quite easy to do when the ham is warm.
5. Now score the fat simply by making cuts with the knife forming a diamond pattern, then stud the centre of each diamond shape with a clove.
6. Cover the fat with the mustard using a palate knife if you have one and, using your hands, finish by covering the mustard with the demerara sugar pressing gently down making sure the sugar sticks.
7. Now wash your hands!
8. Place in preheated oven at 220°C, Gas Mark 7 for about 30 minutes. Keep an eye on it as it will burn easily, turn the roasting tin if necessary.
9. When a golden crust has formed, remove from the oven and allow to rest for a while.
10. Place the ham on a server and soak roasting tin immediately in hot soapy water.
11. Serve hot with celery sauce (recipe further on) or cold, decorated with pineapple rings and cherries for a buffet.

BASIL'S FAVOURITE DINNER

(Serves 4)

This dish is in memory of Basil Gray, a very dear family friend. The Gray family feature a lot in book 1. Sheila is my kind of cook and over the years we have eaten many delicious meals together.

Ingredients:

4 lamb gigot chops
110g/4oz breadcrumbs
55g/2oz melted butter
2 eggs, boiled and grated or chopped
1 garlic clove, crushed
parsley, chopped using scissors

Method:

1. Take a flat baking tray and cover with foil.
2. Lay the chops on the foil.
3. Mix the breadcrumbs, grated eggs, garlic, parsley and melted butter together.
4. Divide mixture between each chop laying it on top to cover.
5. Take another piece of foil and make a lid by placing it on top and sealing the edges.
6. Bake for about 20 minutes at 190°C, Gas Mark 5. Remove foil lid and turn oven down to 150°C, Gas Mark 2 for a further 10-15 minutes making sure lamb is cooked and topping is brown.
7. Serve with mint jelly or mint sauce. Sheila had dauphinoise potatoes with this which was perfect.

SALLY'S CHICKEN TORTILLAS

(Adjust quantities to number you are serving)
By special request from my daughter, Sally. There is no recipe here, just put it all together and of course you can add any other suitable favourite vegetables eg. avocado and salsa.

Ingredients:

1 breaded chicken breast per person
1 onion, sliced thinly
1 each red, green and yellow peppers, sliced
tub of sour cream and chive dip
green salad in a bowl
1 pack of flour tortillas
a little olive oil

Method:

1. Cook chicken according to instructions and cut into strips, place altogether in a wide dish.
2. Heat oil and soften onion, adding peppers to cook and soften too. Put into a serving bowl.
3. Warm tortillas.
4. When you are ready to serve place everything on the table for everyone to help themselves and have fun!

PAPRIKA CHICKEN

(Serves 4, easily doubled)
How did I miss this one out Moira?! Another one of your dinner party specials. I have made this often since. This can be served with roasties which are perfect. You may find you need more sauce so double up on quantities and serve in gravy boat or jug.

Ingredients:

450g/1lb onions, sliced thinly
about 55g/2oz butter
1-2 garlic cloves, chopped finely
4 chicken portions
1 tbsp sweet paprika
150ml/5fl oz/ $\frac{1}{4}$ pint chicken stock
150ml/5fl oz/ $\frac{1}{4}$ pint soured cream
chopped fresh chives (use scissors)
salt and pepper

Method:

1. Preheat oven to 190°C, Gas Mark 5.
2. Melt butter and brown chicken, place in lasagne type dish.
3. Soften onions and garlic in same pan, add paprika, stock and salt and pepper, pour over the chicken.
4. Cover dish and place in oven, middle shelf, for 1 hour.
5. Warm an ashet serving dish and place chicken with sauce in the middle. Pour over the sour cream and scatter with chives.
6. Serve.

CHICKEN, ORANGE AND TARRAGON

(Serves 4)

This recipe has memories of when I was first married. Found in an old recipe book printed in the 70s, I used it over and over in the early days of entertaining because it was so good. If you can get concentrated orange juice all the better (real thick concentrate, it used to be frozen or in tins)

There are two slightly different variations on the same theme.

Recipe 1

Ingredients:

40g/1½oz butter
2 tbsp oil
4 pieces chicken (I use breast but any cut will do)
1 large onion, chopped finely
6¼oz of frozen concentrated orange juice or tin of concentrated orange juice
150ml/5fl oz/ ¼pint water, 1 chicken stock cube
1 tbsp dried or fresh tarragon
15g/ ½oz cornflour (use 1 dessertspoon here)
150ml/5fl oz/ ¼pint carton soured cream or double cream with a dash of lemon juice

Method:

1. Preheat the oven to 180°C, Gas Mark 4.
2 Melt butter with oil in a flameproof casserole dish and brown chicken. Remove and keep to one side.
3 In same oil and butter, soften onion then add orange juice, water, stock cube, and tarragon. Bring to the boil and add chicken.
4. Cover with lid or foil and cook in oven 180°C, Gas Mark 4 for 40-60 minutes (less if you are using chicken breasts). Baste occasionally with sauce.
5. Remove chicken pieces and keep warm. Blend cornflour with 2 tbsp water and add to sauce. Bring to the boil and cook for 2-3 minutes stirring continuously. Cool slightly and stir in cream. Replace chicken back into sauce or serve on an ashet and pour sauce over.

   I serve this with duchesse potatoes to soak up the sauce, carrots and a green vegetable.

Recipe 2

Ingredients:

a knob of butter and a little oil
4 chicken pieces
3-4 shallots (small onions)
1-2 tbsp dried tarragon
2-3 oranges, zest and juice
2 tbsp horseradish cream
300ml/10fl oz/ ½pint double cream

Method:

1. Preheat the oven to 180°C, Gas Mark 4.
2. Melt butter with oil in a flameproof dish and brown chicken.
3. Add shallots, orange juice, zest, horseradish and tarragon.
4. Cover with lid or foil and place in preheated oven for about 20 minutes.
5. Finally add cream and cook for a further 10 minutes.
6. Serve as above

CHICKEN AND BROCCOLI BAKE

(Serves 6-8)
My variation on a very popular dish. I include this because it is so easy and a great prepare ahead meal.

Ingredients:

approx 225g/8oz fresh broccoli, cooked
1 large chicken, cooked and stripped
425g tin condensed chicken soup
4 rounded tbsp real mayonnaise
1 tsp fresh lemon juice
1 tsp Madras curry powder
1 glass sherry

Topping:

55g/2oz Cheddar cheese, grated
about $\frac{1}{2}$ packet cheddar biscuits, crushed

Method:

1. Line wide lasagne type dish with broccoli then lay chicken on top.
2. Mix remaining ingredients together in a bowl and pour over chicken.
3. Sprinkle with cheese and cheddars.
4. Bake in preheated oven 190°C, Gas Mark 5 for 30 minutes until cheese is turning golden brown and is heated through.
5. Serve with a green salad and perhaps crusty bread.

PAN-ROASTED CHICKEN WITH SALAMI

(Serves 6)
Another great all-in-one dish. Sliced salami dry fried makes a lovely crispy topping.

Ingredients:

85g/3oz Milano sliced salami
leaves from 1 large basil plant
3 garlic cloves, crushed
6 chicken breast fillets, with skin
400g can chopped tomatoes
300ml/10fl oz/ $\frac{1}{2}$ pint hot chicken stock
1 small glass red wine
2 tbsp sundried tomato paste
400g can borlotti beans, drained and rinsed
225g/8oz cherry tomatoes, halved

Method:

1. Preheat oven to 200°C, Gas Mark 6.
2. Heat a large flameproof non-stick roasting tin on the hob and drop in the salami slices. Fry for 3-4 minutes until the fat runs off and the salami is crisp. Remove and set aside. Roughly chop half the basil leaves.
3. Add the crushed garlic to the fat in the tin, then fry the chicken breasts two at a time until golden all over. Return all the chicken to the tin and stir in the tomatoes, stock,

See over for Method

wine, tomato paste, chopped basil and beans. Season with salt and freshly ground pepper. Bring to the boil, then cover with foil and transfer the roasting tin to the oven for 20 minutes.

4. Uncover the chicken, scatter over the cherry tomatoes and return to the oven for a further 15 minutes. Adjust the seasoning, then scatter over the crispy salami and remaining basil leaves before serving.

CHICKEN WITH BOURSIN, SERVED WITH WILD RICE, COURGETTES AND CASHEW NUTS AND ROASTED RED PEPPERS

(Serves 6)

Ah!!! Again memories of my Dad. He gave me a Woman and Home Diary for Christmas in 1983 and this recipe with the serving accompaniments was in it. I have served it and shared it with many friends. The dish can all be prepared in the morning and it looks very impressive when served.

Ingredients for chicken:

3 tbsp olive oil
6 chicken breasts, without skin
175g/6oz Boursin cheese with garlic and herbs
salt and pepper
6 tbsp white wine
$1\frac{1}{2}$ tbsp lemon juice
20g/ $\frac{3}{4}$ oz butter
30g/$1\frac{1}{4}$ oz fresh white breadcrumbs
1-2 tbsp freshly chopped or dried herbs
300ml/10fl oz/ $\frac{1}{2}$ pint double cream

Method:

1. Start by heating 2 tbsp olive oil in a frying pan and browning the chicken breasts on each side. Remove from pan and drain on kitchen paper.
2. Using a sharp knife slit down the side of each breast to form a pocket and insert Boursin cheese. (Divide cheese equally between the breasts)
3. Lay the chicken in an ovenproof dish and drizzle over the wine and lemon juice, salt and black pepper. Cover with foil and keep in fridge until ready to cook in oven 200°C, Gas Mark 6 for about 20-25 minutes.
4. Also prepare the topping ahead. Don't wash the frying pan but add the last 1 tbsp olive oil and 30g/$1\frac{1}{4}$oz butter to melt.
5. Add the breadcrumbs to brown, not burn, drain on kitchen paper and put in small dish.
6. When breadcrumbs are cool add the chopped mixed herbs, mix, cover and leave at the side for later.
7. When you are ready to serve, have the plates in the oven heating. Remove the sauce from the chicken and put into a small saucepan, keeping chicken warm. Simmer the sauce for a few minutes to reduce in volume and then add the cream. Heat through.
8. Place the chicken at the side of a warm plate, pour some sauce over and then a teaspoon of the breadcrumb mixture on top. Serve at once with the wild rice and red peppers at the side. They go perfectly together and I guarantee a spotless plate.

Roasted red peppers

There are a few ways to roast peppers but this way I find the easiest for this recipe. Again prepare ahead.

Ingredients:

4 large red peppers
1 onion, sliced
1 garlic clove, crushed
a little olive oil

Method:

1. Put on the grill to heat up. Place whole peppers under the grill and allow to go blackish and wrinkly all over, by turning periodically with the stalk.
2. When the peppers have generally softened, place them in a polythene bag and allow them to cool down. This will help them shrink and become easier to handle and the skin to peel off.
3. Remove stalk, seeds, skin and then slice.
4. Heat a little olive oil in a small saucepan and soften onion and garlic. Add the peppers. Keep to one side to reheat later.
5. When ready to serve the meal, heat the peppers through and divide between the hot plates alongside the chicken and rice.

Wild rice with courgette and toasted cashew nuts

Again toast the nuts ahead (see note below) and dice the courgette, cover and leave until ready to cook the rice.

Ingredients:

175g/6oz wild and long grain rice- it comes mixed in a box
1 courgette, diced
55g/2oz toasted cashew nuts- see note below

Method:

1. Cook the rice according to instructions on box and add diced courgette to last 3 minutes of cooking time.
2. Drain and stir in cashew nuts.
3. Serve on the side with the chicken and peppers.

Note: to toast the nuts place on a small baking tray or plate under a hot grill and keep a good eye on them as they burn easily. Toasting improves the flavour and is well worth doing.

EASY SPICED CHICKEN

(Serves 4)
Another easy one, recommended by Janie, and it is good!

Ingredients:

olive oil
4 chicken breasts, sliced
2 onions
1 jar of tomato pickle
1 tsp each of curry powder, turmeric, cumin, paprika, ground coriander
1 dessertspoon plain flour
approx.150ml/5fl oz/ ¼ pint chicken stock

Method:

1. Heat a little oil in pan and brown sliced chicken. Remove chicken from pan and keep to one side.
2. Add about 1 tbsp oil to pan and soften onion.
3. Add flour and spices to make a roux, then slowly add chicken stock adding more liquid if needed to make a smooth sauce. Don't panic if it gets lumpy, just use a whisk to remove lumps. Continue stirring to cook for a few minutes.
4. Add chicken and heat through.
5. Serve with rice, poppadums, and mango chutney.

GRILLED CHICKEN WITH SWEET CHILLI SAUCE

(Serves 4)
Low fat, with lovely flavours. Serve with potato wedges and light sour cream and chive dip.

Ingredients:

4 skinless chicken breasts
2 tbsp olive oil
1 tbsp fresh rosemary or marjoram, finely chopped
2 tbsp sweet chilli sauce
1 tbsp freshly squeezed lime juice

Method:

1. Slice each chicken breast in half horizontally, leaving it attached along one side - you should be able to open it out like a book. Flatten with the palms of your hands to make sure the halves are roughly the same thickness.
2. Mix the olive oil and rosemary or marjoram in a shallow dish. Season the chicken with salt and freshly ground black pepper and coat evenly with the herb oil. Leave to marinade until ready to cook.
3. Cook on a preheated grill pan or barbecue for 3-4 minutes each side, depending on the thickness, until cooked through - there should be no pink juices.
4. Mix the sweet chilli sauce with the lime juice. Serve the chicken straightaway drizzled with sauce.

STUFFED CHICKEN ALL-IN-ONE DISH

(Serves 4)

I have used this recipe often especially when the girls were both at school. We all love it. It is all cooked together in the oven and then dished up on one big platter and placed in the middle of the table for everyone to help themselves. Looks impressive.

Ingredients:

2 spring onions
85g/3oz canned pineapple
salt and ground black pepper
4 chicken supremes or fillets with skin
110ml/4fl oz bought barbecue sauce or tomato ketchup
50ml/2fl oz maple syrup
2 tbsp distilled malt vinegar
2 tsp lemon juice
2 garlic cloves
6 tbsp olive oil
4 small red onions, about 225g/8oz total weight
450g/1lb small red potatoes
flat-leaf parsley to garnish

Method:

1. Finely chop the spring onions and pineapple. Mix them together and season. Make a shallow pocket in the thickest part of each supreme. Place a little of the mixture in the pocket and fold it over to enclose. Fasten with a wooden cocktail stick and set aside.
2. Blend together the barbecue sauce, maple syrup, vinegar, lemon juice, crushed garlic cloves and 5tbsp oil. Place the chicken in a shallow, non-metallic dish and pour over half the marinade. Cover and leave to marinade overnight.
3. Peel and quarter the red onions. Quarter the potatoes and toss in the remaining olive oil. Spread over the base of a large roasting tin. Cook at 230°C, Gas Mark 8 for 45 minutes, turning from time to time.
4. Sit the chicken on the vegetables and pour over the remaining marinade. Cook at 230°C, Gas Mark 8 for 30-35 minutes or until the chicken is tender and everything is golden brown.
5. Carefully remove the cocktail sticks and lift the chicken and vegetables on to a serving dish. Cover and keep warm. Add 4-6 tbsp water to the pan juices and bring to the boil. Spoon the barbecue sauce over the chicken and serve, garnished with sprigs of flat-leaf parsley.

SALMON WITH STIR-FRY VEGETABLES

(Serves 4)
Low fat, easy and impressive. A magazine cut out.

Ingredients:

4 pieces salmon fillet
110g/4oz mangetout
2 carrots, peeled
2 tsp sesame oil
110g/4oz beansprouts
2 tsp toasted sesame seeds
6 tbsp soy sauce
2 tbsp runny honey
small piece of root ginger, peeled
1 lemon

Method:

1. Preheat the oven to 190°C, Gas Mark 5. Slice the root ginger into matchsticks. Thinly slice the lemon. Cut four 23cm/9 inch square pieces of greaseproof paper; place a few lemon slices in the centre of each sheet. Top with a salmon fillet, scatter on some ginger.
2. Fold the greaseproof paper over the salmon. Pinch the edges together to make a parcel. Place on a large baking sheet. Bake for 20-25 minutes until the salmon is just cooked. Finely shred the mangetout and pare the carrots into thin strips.
3. Heat the sesame oil in a wok. Stir-fry the mangetout, carrots and beansprouts for 3-4 minutes. Put the salmon on serving plates and pile the stir-fried vegetables on top. Sprinkle with sesame seeds. Heat the soy sauce and honey in the wok and pour over the salmon and vegetables.

VEGETABLE AND CRANBERRY PUFF PASTRY PIE

(Serves 8)
This recipe was given to me by Morag with whom I have worked for many years. She has a family of vegetarians and this is a great favourite. I like the puff pastry but Morag prefers to use filo pastry.

Ingredients:

1 tbsp soya or vegetable oil
2 garlic cloves, crushed
1 small onion, finely chopped
1 medium red or green pepper, deseeded and finely chopped
2 carrots, grated
50g/1¾oz button mushrooms, sliced
75g/2¾oz peanuts, roughly chopped
50g/1¾oz hazelnuts, roughly chopped
50g/1¾oz brown breadcrumbs, wholemeal or granary
2 tomatoes, chopped
1 egg, beaten
2 tsp dried parsley
450g/1lb puff pastry
4 tbsp cranberry sauce
1 tbsp milk
salt and pepper

Method:

1. Preheat the oven to 200°C, Gas Mark 6.
2. Heat the oil in a large pan and fry the garlic, onion and pepper for 5 minutes until softened.
3. Add the carrots and button mushrooms and stir for another 2 minutes.
4. Stir in all the remaining ingredients except the cranberry sauce, puff pastry and milk, season to taste and stir well.
5. Roll out half the pastry on a lightly floured board to a 25cm x 15cm/10 x 6 inch rectangle.
6. Place half of the filling on the pastry leaving a 1cm/ ½ inch border. Spread the cranberry sauce over the filling and top with the remaining filling.
7. Roll out the second piece of pastry, enough to cover the filling. Trim the edges with a knife and crimp firmly. Place on a baking tray and brush with milk, cook in the oven for 35-40 minutes until golden and well risen.

Note: If you decide to try filo pastry, use a large flan dish bringing the pastry up the sides and scrunch the filo pastry over the top. Cooking time is the same.

SAUSAGE MEATBALLS AND BOSTON BAKED BEANS

(Serves 6)
This is a great tasting all-in-one dish to make ahead and looks impressive. All this needs is crusty bread to serve.

Ingredients:

For the meatballs:
750g/1lb 10oz good quality coarse sausages
4 tbsp chopped flat-leaf parsley
2 tbsp freshly chopped oregano or 1 level tsp dried oregano
salt and freshly ground pepper
3 tbsp oil

For the Boston baked beans:
3 x 420g cans cannelloni beans
2 tbsp oil
1 medium onion
3 level tbsp plain flour
150ml/5fl oz/ ¼ pint vegetable stock
2 x 400g cans chopped tomatoes
3 tbsp Dijon mustard
3 level tbsp soft light brown sugar
2 tbsp black treacle
3 tbsp Worcestershire sauce
1 tbsp white wine vinegar
salt and freshly ground pepper
4 tbsp soured cream
55g/2oz Cheddar cheese
oregano sprigs to garnish

See over for Method

Method:

1. To make the meatballs, slit the sausage skins with a small sharp knife and squeeze the meat into a large bowl. With your hands, mix in the herbs and seasoning. Shape the meat into 18 balls, put on a baking sheet, then cover and chill for 20 minutes.
2. Meanwhile, make the Boston baked beans. Rinse and drain the beans, then heat the oil in a pan, chop the onion and cook for 5 minutes until softened. Stir in the flour and cook for a further minute. Add the stock, stirring until smooth, then add the chopped tomatoes, mustard, sugar, treacle, Worcestershire sauce, white wine vinegar and beans. Season, then bring slowly to the boil, stirring constantly. Pour into a shallow 2.8 litre/ 5 pint ovenproof dish.
3. Heat the oil for the meatballs in a large frying pan and fry them in batches for 2 minutes until lightly browned. Put them on absorbent kitchen paper and keep to one side until all the meatballs are cooked.
4. Add the meatballs to the beans, turning to coat in the bean mixture and cook at 180°C, Gas Mark 4 for 40-45 minutes or until bubbling. Drizzle with the soured cream, sprinkle with grated cheese, then grill until golden. Garnish with oregano.

DINNER PARTY BEEF

(Serves 4)

Dinner party material, a recipe from long ago entertaining. It was always enjoyed.

Ingredients:

1kg/2lb 4oz braising steak, trimmed and cut into 8 even-sized pieces
salt and black pepper
2 tbsp oil
2 onions, peeled and sliced
1 garlic clove, peeled and crushed
2 tbsp flour
150ml/5fl oz/ ¼pt red wine
150ml/5fl oz/ ¼pt beef stock
425g/15oz can tomatoes
1 tbsp tomato purée
2 tbsp capers, optional
1 tbsp wine vinegar
sprigs of parsley to garnish

Method:

1. Preheat oven to 180°C, Gas Mark 4.
2. Sprinkle the meat with salt and pepper. Heat 1 tbsp of the oil in a pan and fry the beef until well sealed all over. Transfer to a casserole.
3. Add the remaining oil to the pan and fry the onions and garlic until lightly browned.
4. Stir in the flour and cook for 1 minute, then gradually add the wine, stock and juice from the tomatoes and bring to the boil for 2 minutes. Add the tomato purée, capers if using, vinegar and plenty of salt and pepper then pour over the beef and add the tomatoes.
5. Cover the casserole and cook in a preheated oven for 2-2½ hours or until tender. Taste and adjust the seasoning.
6. Serve garnished with parsley.

BEEF WITH LAGER AND SWEET POTATO TOPPING

(Serves 6)

A wonderful all-in-one dish. If you have never bought or eaten sweet potato this is the dish to make. Your guests will be impressed. Serve simply with a green vegetable. Suitable for freezing without the potato topping.

Ingredients:

3 tbsp olive oil
900g/2 lb braising steak, diced
1 large red onion, sliced into chunky wedges
2 garlic cloves, crushed
225g/8oz chestnut mushrooms, halved, or quartered if large
40g/1½oz plain flour
300ml/10fl oz/ ½pt lager
150ml/5fl oz/ ¼pt beef stock
1 tbsp tomato purée
1 tbsp light brown sugar
175g/6oz sundried tomatoes, each one snipped into four
salt and pepper

Topping:
450g/1lb sweet potatoes
450g/1lb old potatoes

Method:

1. Heat 2 tbsps of the oil in a large casserole dish. Fry the meat over a high heat until browned all over (you may need to do this in batches). Remove the meat from the pan with a slotted spoon and set aside.
2. Add the remaining oil to the same pan, along with the onion, garlic and mushrooms, and fry over a high heat for a few minutes.
3. Return the meat to the pan, sprinkle in the flour, then gradually blend in the lager and stock, mixing continuously over a high heat until smooth.
4. Bring to the boil and add the remaining ingredients and salt and pepper.
5. Cover, place in oven and cook at 160°C, Gas Mark 3 for about 1½ hours or until the meat is tender. Taste for seasoning and set aside until cold.
6. For the topping, peel both lots of potatoes and cut into even-sized chunks. Cook in boiling salted water until tender, then drain and mash with salt and pepper to taste.
7. Once the casserole is cold, tip into a deep ovenproof dish of about 1.7 litre/3 pint capacity (not too wide) and top with the potato topping. Bake in an oven preheated to 200°C, Gas Mark 6 for about 30-40 minutes until piping hot.

DEBBIE'S CASSEROLE

(Serves 6)

Remember this one Debbie? You used this one for entertaining us on more than one occasion and there was never a bit left.

Ingredients:

685g/1½ lbs of braising steak, sliced
295g tin condensed mushroom soup
2 onions, sliced
1 tsp made English mustard
5 tsp horseradish sauce
1 tsp Lea and Perrins sauce
110g/4oz mushrooms, sliced (optional)
oil

Method:

1. Heat oil and soften onions.
2. Add meat and brown.
3. Add mustard, horseradish, Lea and Perrins and coat the meat, then pour over soup.
4. Cook in preheated oven 180°C, Gas Mark 4 for 1½ hours.
5. Add sliced mushrooms if using, cook for a further 30 minutes.
6. This can be served with rice or creamy potatoes.

SALADS & VEGETABLES

TURKEY SLICES

(Serves 10)

Very impressive buffet dish. Great fun to put together. Make sure the foil is well sealed before putting it in the oven.

Ingredients:

225g/8oz smoked rindless bacon
6 boneless, skinless, turkey breast portions
1 bunch fresh tarragon
4tbsp double cream or crème fraîche
4 x 75g/2¾oz packets of garlic and herb cheese, ie Boursin
3tbsp Dijon mustard
225g/8oz wafer-thin smoked ham

Method:

1. Place a double sheet of foil on a work surface. Stretch out bacon rashers using the back of a knife and arrange, just over-lapping, on the foil. Arrange turkey on top, cover with clingfilm and flatten with a rolling pin.
2. Remove the clingfilm and scatter the tarragon leaves over the turkey breasts. Blend cream or crème fraîche with the garlic and herb cheese and spread evenly over the turkey with a palette knife.
3. Thinly spread the mustard over the cheese mixture. Arrange ham slices in ruffles along the centre, leaving a 5cm/ 2 inch border of uncovered mustard on the long edges – this will make rolling easier.
4. Lift foil along the longest edge and use to roll up turkey tightly. Roll foil edges together to secure them keeping turkey tightly wrapped. Bake at 200°C, Gas Mark 6 for 1hr 15minutes.
5. Cool until completely cold and chill. Slice to serve.

ASIAN RICE SALAD

(Serves 12)

This goes with the fish tart and coronation chicken. You can complete this dish the day before. Add the mint just before serving.

Ingredients:

300g/10½oz basmati and wild rice
200g/7oz green beans
125g/4 ½oz asparagus tips
150g/5½oz sugar snap peas
450g/1lb cooked king prawns
5 tbsp chopped fresh mint

For the dressing:
juice of 3 limes
4 tbsp sweet chilli sauce
1 tbsp Thai fish sauce

Method:

1. Wash the rice, then place in a large sauté pan with 600ml/1 pint cold water. Bring to the boil, simmer and cover – the rice is cooked when all the water has evaporated. Turn off the heat and leave to steam. Let it get completely cold then chill.

2. Blanch the green beans, asparagus tips and sugar snaps in a pan of boiling water until they are just tender, then quickly refresh under cold running water.
3. Mix together the dressing ingredients and stir into the rice. To assemble, add the rest of the ingredients, except the mint to the rice and mix well. Chill until needed, then add the mint.

ROCKET, BABY GEM AND AVOCADO SALAD WITH PARMESAN CROUTÔNS

(serves 8- 10)

Ingredients:

1/2 ciabatta loaf, cut into cubes
5 tbsp olive oil
4 tbsp grated fresh Parmesan
3 baby gem lettuces, leaves separated
150g/5 1/2 oz rocket
2 avocados, peeled and thickly sliced
2-3 tbsp pumpkin seeds, toasted
Parmesan shavings, to serve

For the lemon dressing:
2 tsp Dijon mustard
2 tsp honey
juice of 1/2 a lemon
5 tbsp olive oil
6 basil leaves, torn

Method:

1. Preheat the oven to 180°C, Gas Mark 4. Mix the ciabatta in a bowl with the oil, Parmesan and black pepper. Put onto a baking sheet and bake for 15 minutes until golden.
2. Mix the dressing ingredients and season. Mix together the salad ingredients and sprinkle over the dressing and Parmesan.

Note: If the salad is going to be on the table for quite a while, serve the dressing separately to prevent the rocket going soggy. Prepare the croutôns the day before and keep in an airtight container.

CHICKEN, PRAWN, MANGO AND AVOCADO SALAD WITH GINGER LIME DRESSING

(Serves 4)
Found this recipe in a magazine whilst waiting for the dentist, as you do! The ingredients were enough to make me love it, and I do.

Ingredients:

2 cooked chicken breasts, sliced
200g/7oz cooked, peeled prawns
1 ripe avocado, sliced

See over for Method

1 ripe mango, sliced or diced (remembering to cut longitudinally as the stone is round and thin)
¼ cucumber, peeled and chopped
4 gem lettuce, leaves separated
110g/4oz toasted cashew nuts (see below)

Dressing:
Make in empty jam jar or whisk together in a mug

1 lime, zest and juice
2 tsp white wine vinegar
½ tsp fresh ginger, grated
3 tbsp extra virgin olive oil
salt and pepper

Method:
1. Place chicken in bowl with avocado, mango, prawns and cucumber. Mix gently.
2. Divide the lettuce between the plates and lay on mixture.
3. Drizzle on dressing finishing off with the nuts.
4. Serve.

Note: To toast cashew nuts, place them on a baking tray under a hot grill and keep a good eye on them turning occasionally, as they brown easily. The flavour is greatly enhanced.

CORONATION CHICKEN
(Serves 12)
The easy yummy alternative to the real version in book 1. You can make the dressing and mix up the chicken the day before, but add the spring onions and coriander just before serving and garnishing.

Ingredients:
2 small to medium cooked chickens, stripped off the bone
75g/2 ¾ oz pine nuts, toasted
50g/1¾ oz sultanas
100g/3½ oz dried apricots, chopped
1 bunch spring onions, finely chopped
4 tbsp chopped fresh coriander
1 bag baby salad leaves

For the dressing:
1½ tbsp Madras curry paste
100ml/3½ fl oz mayonnaise
200ml/7fl oz natural or Greek yogurt (not low fat)
3 tbsp mango chutney
squeeze fresh lemon juice

Method:
1. Mix together all the ingredients for the dressing and add freshly ground black pepper. In a large bowl, mix together the chicken, pine nuts (reserving a few), sultanas, apricots and half the spring onions and coriander.
2. Stir in the dressing. Put the salad leaves on a platter, spoon over the chicken mix, then scatter over remaining pine nuts, spring onions and coriander.

DAUPHINOISE POTATOES

(Serves 4)
I love the aroma in the kitchen as this cooks. This is easily made, but only for special occasions.

Ingredients:

685g/1½lb large potatoes
1 garlic clove, crushed
175ml/6fl oz milk
75ml/2½fl oz double cream
about 25g/1oz Parmesan cheese, grated
salt

Method:

1. Preheat oven to 180°C, Gas Mark 4.
2. Very, very thinly slice potatoes. (Takes time but is well worth it)
3. In a large pan place potato slices, milk, garlic and about 2 tsp of salt. Mix gently. Put on lid and slowly bring to the boil checking occasionally and stirring carefully.
4. Add cream and cook for a further few minutes, stirring until the starch combines with the milk and cream and a thick sauce forms.
5. Transfer everything to a gratin dish and sprinkle with the Parmesan cheese.
6. Bake in the oven for about 45 minutes until potatoes are browned and cooked.

POTATO WEDGES

Adjust quantities as required.
I make this often, in fact I hardly ever cook frozen chips. These are much healthier and taste great with a dip.

Ingredients:

large baking potato or biggish potatoes allowing 1 per person
olive oil
herbs, garlic or paprika (optional)
salt and pepper

Method:

1. Wash and dry potato, leaving skin on or removing as preferred and cut into half down the middle then each half into four wedges.
2. Toss in olive oil in roasting tin.
3. Add herbs, crushed garlic or paprika if using, and salt and pepper.
4. Place in hot oven 200 -220°C, Gas Mark 6-7 for 30-35 minutes.
5. Serve stacked on plates individually or in ramekins with dip or tomato sauce.

ROAST POTATOES

Adjust quantities as required.
Not difficult but I have put the method in to help you achieve crispy roasties.

Ingredients:

allow 1 large potato per person with an extra one thrown in.
sunflower oil

See over for Method

Method:

1. Peel and cut potatoes into four, place in large saucepan, cover with cold water and bring to boil. Allow to boil for approximately 5 minutes only.
2. Drain off water and shake potatoes in the pan with a lid. Cover with clean tea towel or kitchen roll to dry off. This can be done a few hours before you want to cook.
3. Place roasting dish in oven, top shelf with a good glug of oil. Heat oven to 220°C, Gas Mark 7 for 15-20 minutes.
4. When oil is very hot carefully lift out tray and toss potatoes in the oil. Replace back into oven for around 30-40 minutes.
5. Check occasionally and turn the potatoes around so they get even browning. You may have to turn up your oven.
6. Serve in warm dish.

DUCHESSE POTATOES

Adjust quantities as required.

Dinner party potatoes. To be really organised, these can be prepared early in the day and no dirty saucepan to wash up when you are busy. I would recommend you buy the disposable piping bags in Lakeland Plastics for this recipe and, I can assure you, they will come in very useful. Share a pack with a friend.

Ingredients:

allow 1 big potato per person, or two smaller, plus an extra to make sure you have plenty
a knob of butter and a little milk
a good grinding of black pepper
a piping bag and plain or fancy nozzle, those ones used for piping cream (optional)

Method:

1. Peel and boil potatoes until soft.
2. Mash well, no lumps, with butter and milk, salt and pepper.
3. Allow to cool slightly if you are going to pipe.
4. Pipe in a rosette shape or use a spoon and fork to place approximately a dessert spoon amount on a baking tray, allowing two per person. Make a neat shape if using a fork.
5. Cool and cover until ready to heat through.
6. Place in preheated oven 200°C, Gas Mark 6 for about 20 minutes until they are going brown at the edges.

MINI ROASTIES

Adjust quantities as required.

Using old or new potatoes I use this method just for a change.

Ingredients:

allow 1 big potato per person or use a bag of new potatoes with extra thrown in
a knob of butter and extra virgin olive oil
1 garlic clove, crushed (optional)
fresh herbs such as rosemary, thyme or chives or dried herbs (optional)
salt and pepper

Method:

1. Wash and dry the potatoes thoroughly leaving skins on and cut into largish chunks or leave new potatoes as they are, depending on size.
2. Place oil and butter into roasting tin and heat up in hot oven 220°C, Gas Mark 7.
3. Toss the potatoes in the oil and butter, adding the garlic, salt and pepper and dried herbs if using.
4. Cook until they are looking cooked and crispy, usually about 30-40 minutes.
5. If you are using fresh herbs toss them with the potatoes and serve.

BARBECUE SAUCE

(Serves 4)

Got this recipe years ago from Chrissie. I usually marinade chicken thighs or breasts in it then serve with the fried rice.

Ingredients:

1 tsp mustard powder
1 tsp ground ginger
2 tbsp caster sugar
1 tbsp Lea and Perrins sauce
1 tbsp tomato purée
3-4 tbsp fresh orange juice
dash of soya sauce
salt and pepper

Method:

Whisk all together in a bowl and use to marinade or pour over chicken pieces and roast in the oven for around 25 minutes 200°C, Gas Mark 6.

FRIED RICE

(Serves 4)

Easy and straightforward.

Ingredients:

175g/6oz (uncooked weight) rice, either white or brown, easy cook
110g/4oz frozen peas
3 tbsp oil
2 onions, thinly sliced
4 rashers bacon, chopped (I use kitchen scissors to do this, much easier).
3 eggs, beaten
salt and pepper

Method:

1. Cook rice. Many people have a panic cooking rice. I usually do mine in the microwave and never have any problems. The biggest tip is to use lots of boiling water in a big bowl and cook for the recommended time, then drain. Remember brown rice does take longer.
2. This can be cooked ahead, remembering to rinse with cold water to separate the

See over for Method

3. Meanwhile melt butter in a pan and cook peas. The butter produces more flavour but you can simply boil the peas in water if you prefer. Drain and keep to one side.
4. When you are ready to serve, take a big frying pan or a wok, heat oil, soften onions and cook bacon.
5. Add beaten eggs to pan stirring with wooden spoon to scramble. Just as the eggs start to set, quickly add the cooked rice allowing the eggs to set around grains and keep stirring.
6. Finally add cooked peas and a little salt and pepper to taste.
7. Serve.

GENOVESE PASTA SALAD

(Serves 8-10)
Colourful!

Ingredients:

350g/12oz pasta spirals (mixed colours)
1 red pepper, diced
1 green pepper, diced
1 yellow pepper, diced
homemade or shop bought vinaigrette dressing with 2 tsp pesto sauce added to about
$^1\!/_2$ a bottle (approx 125ml/4fl oz)

Method:

1. Cook pasta according to instructions and toss in dressing while still warm.
2. Allow to go cold and then add peppers, chill.
3. Serve.

BEAN SALAD

(Serves 8-10)
Used often in cold buffets, easy.

Ingredients:

small bag frozen green beans, cooked
2 tins kidney beans, drained
2 tins broad beans, drained
1 onion, sliced thinly
1 green pepper, sliced thinly

Dressing:
Make in an empty jam jar.

$^1\!/_4$-$^1\!/_2$ cup caster sugar
$^1\!/_2$ cup white wine vinegar
$^1\!/_3$ cup olive oil
salt and pepper
parsley, chopped to garnish

Method:

1. Simply put all dressing ingredients in a jar and shake.
2. Mix all main ingredients together in a bowl and add dressing, mix well but carefully.
3. Chill until required, decorate with parsley.

COLESLAW WITHOUT MAYONNAISE

(Serves 8)

This recipe was given to me by Catriona, as a request when I was cooking for her daughter's Christening. Grandad didn't like mayonnaise in his coleslaw so this was the alternative.

Ingredients:

450g/1lb white cabbage, finely sliced
225g/8oz carrots, grated
110g/4oz spring onions, chopped
1 red apple, finely sliced
125ml/4fl oz olive oil
50ml/2fl oz grape seed oil, or any nut oil
juice of 1 lemon
1 garlic clove
1 heaped tsp runny honey
1 tsp Dijon mustard
salt and pepper

Method:

1. Mix all ingredients together.
2. Add apple before serving.

MARINATED MUSHROOM SALAD

(Serves 8)

A little bit different.

Ingredients:

225g/8oz closed cup mushrooms
1 stick celery, sliced
1 spring onion, sliced
1 tbsp chopped parsley (use scissors)

Dressing:
Make in an empty jam jar

2 tbsp sunflower oil
1 tbsp sherry
1 garlic clove, crushed
1 tsp soft brown sugar

Method:

1. Simply put all dressing ingredients in the jar and shake.
2. Wipe and trim mushrooms, cut big ones in half.
3. Place in bowl with remaining ingredients, add dressing and mix well.
4. Chill 2-24 hours.
5. Serve.

CELERY SAUCE

This is a must with the baked ham. It can be made hours before, covered and reheated when ready to serve.

Method:

1. Dice and boil a $\frac{1}{2}$ head of celery. Drain.
2. Melt about 55g/2oz of butter in a pan and sauté the celery for a few minutes.
3. Add 55g/2oz flour and about $\frac{1}{2}$ pint of a mixture of chicken stock and milk. Stir till smooth.
4. Liquidise. Add a teaspoon of lemon juice and a pinch of nutmeg.
5. Season.

CREAMED TURNIP

Method:

1. Boil your turnip as normal until soft. Drain.
2. Chop some bacon and sauté in a pan with a knob of butter.
3. Return the turnip to the pan, mash and mix well with bacon.
4. Add a couple of tablespoons of cream, salt and pepper and keep mixing and mashing - yummy!

GLAZED CARROTS AND PARSNIPS

This is a prepare-ahead vegetable and has lovely flavours.

Ingredients:

700g /1lb 9oz each of carrots and parsnips, halved lengthways
zest and juice of a lemon
2 tbsp light muscovado sugar
25g/1oz butter
450ml/15fl oz/ $\frac{3}{4}$ pint hot vegetable stock using one vegetable cube
2 tbsp chives, chopped using scissors

Method:

1. Cook carrots and parsnips in large pan of boiling water for 2-3 minutes. Drain well.
2. Tip the vegetables into a large roasting tin and add the remaining ingredients except the chives. Season and then cover with foil.
3. This can then be chilled until ready to cook.
4. Cook in the oven at 190°C, Gas Mark 5 for 30 minutes then remove foil and cook for a further 10 minutes.
5. Drain, reserving stock and keep or use to add to sauce or gravy. Stir in chives and serve in a warm serving dish.

DESSERTS

FUDGE CHEESECAKE

(Serves 8)

It is absolutely magic! This will be the one you will make for Christmas and lots of special occasions. It came from Sue Lawrence's book 'A Cook's tour of Scotland'; Sue's recipe was from Orkney and uses Orkney fudge, but I have made a few changes to suit my taste.

Ingredients:

250g/9oz Hobnobs (or other oaty biscuits), crushed
75g/2³/₄oz butter, melted
300g/10¹/₂oz Philadelphia cream cheese
250g/9oz fudge
450ml/16fl oz double cream, lightly whipped
Dulce de Leche toffee sauce, to decorate

Method:

1. Lightly butter a 24cm/9¹/₂inch springform cake tin. Make the base by combining the biscuits and butter, and pressing into the base of the prepared tin.
2. Beat the cream cheese until soft.
3. Melt 200g/7oz of the fudge by placing in a bowl in the microwave for about 1 minute, or until soft (or in a pan over a very low heat), so that when you stir it becomes a soft paste. You do not want it to be hot, only warm. Stir in the cream cheese beating until combined, then gently fold in the cream.
4. Spoon onto the biscuit base, smoothing the top, and chill for at least 6 hours before serving.
5. Chop the remaining fudge and keep to one side.
6. When ready to serve sprinkle fudge on top and drizzle with Dulce de Leche.

TIRAMISU

(Serves 10-14)

This feeds a lot of people, great for a buffet and so easy. No cooking just putting together. Suitable for freezing at stage 4.

Ingredients:

175g/6oz good quality plain chocolate
300g/10oz Madeira cake
150ml/5fl oz/ ¹/₄pint strong black coffee
5 tbsp Tia Maria or dark rum or brandy
3 x 250g/9oz tubs of mascarpone
85g/3oz caster sugar
430ml/15fl oz/ ³/₄pint double cream
85g/3oz amaretti biscuits
icing sugar for dusting

Method:

1. Use the coarse side of a grater to grate all the chocolate for the layers and top.
2. Line the base and sides of a 20cm/8 inch round loose bottomed cake tin with cling film. Cut the cake into 20 thin slices and use half to line the bottom of the tin, cutting the cake to fit neatly so there are no gaps.

3. Mix the coffee with the Tia Maria and sprinkle about $\frac{1}{3}$ of the liquid over the cake, beat together two of the tubs of mascarpone with 55g/2oz of sugar. Whip 300ml/ $\frac{1}{2}$ pint of the cream and fold into the mixture. Spoon half this mixture over the cake base spreading evenly with back of metal spoon. Sprinkle with half the grated chocolate.
4. Crumble the amaretti into small pieces and scatter evenly over the chocolate. Cover with the last pieces of Madeira cake - again cutting to fit. Sprinkle with the rest of the coffee. Cover the top with clingfilm and chill overnight or freeze. Chill remaining chocolate on a separate plate covered loosely with cling.
5. Up to 2 hours before serving uncover the cake and invert it onto a flat serving plate. Carefully remove the tin and peel off the clingfilm. Soften the remaining mascarpone and the remaining sugar, whip the rest of the cream and fold into the mix. Spread this mixture over the top and sides of the cake then sprinkle the top with the remaining chocolate. Dust lightly with the icing sugar and cut into slices.

CRUMBLED TOP APPLE PIE

(Serves 8-10)
Variation on a theme given to me when I catered for a friend's Christening. Suitable for freezing.

Ingredients:
a 23cm/9 inch shortcrust pastry base, frozen or homemade (see Lemon Meringue Pie recipe)

Filling:
700g/1lb 9oz Bramley apples
25g/1oz soft brown sugar
$\frac{1}{4}$ tsp ground cloves
$\frac{1}{2}$ tsp ground cinnamon
75g/$2\frac{3}{4}$oz raisins
2 tbsps water
$\frac{1}{4}$ whole nutmeg, grated

Crumble topping:
50g/$1\frac{3}{4}$oz self raising flour
25g/1oz demerara sugar
110g/4oz pecan nuts or walnuts, chopped
75g/$2\frac{3}{4}$oz firm butter (important or it goes all soggy!)
pinch each of ground nutmeg, ginger and cinnamon

Method:
1. Make pastry and bake blind (see method in Lemon Meringue Pie).
2. Prepare apples and add to pan with other ingredients. Cook gently for about 10 minutes. Cool.
3. For crumble topping, rub butter into flour, using cool hands until mixture resembles breadcrumbs and add remaining ingredients. Or if you have a food processor simply mix all ingredients together using a pulse action until you have a coarse crumble.
4. Add apples to pastry base, sprinkle over crumble topping and cook in a moderate oven, 180°C, Gas Mark 4 for about 20-30 minutes.

STRAWBERRY SHORTCAKE

(Serves 6 - 8)
So easy and looks impressive. This has got to be the most asked-for recipe this summer. As you read through the ingredients and find out how simple it is to make you will see why. Suitable for freezing.

Ingredients:

25g/1oz butter
200g/7oz shortbread, crushed
150g/5½oz white chocolate
300ml/ ½pint double cream, lightly whipped
225g/8oz strawberries or raspberries, chopped

Method:

1. Melt butter and stir in crushed shortbread.
2. Melt chocolate, whip cream and fold in melted chocolate.
3. Put half the shortbread mix into a 20cm/8 inch loose bottom tin and press mixture down slightly with fingers.
4. Spread half chocolate/cream mix on top of shortbread followed by fruit and remainder of chocolate/cream mix.
5. Spread remainder of shortbread mix on top and flatten slightly.

CAPPUCCINO CHOC POTS

(Serves 6)
You will make this over and over. The cream sits on top of the pudding and makes a lovely contrast of colour. The simplicity, overall taste and presentation in champagne flutes makes it a winner.

Ingredients:

125ml/4fl oz very strong black coffee
2 tbsp brandy
225g/8oz good quality plain chocolate, broken into pieces
55g/2oz caster sugar
300ml/ ½pint double cream
110g/4oz mascarpone (or fromage frais)
18 ratafia biscuits
4 tbsp orange juice

To finish:
6 tbsp double cream
25g/1oz plain chocolate, grated or shaved into small curls

Method:

1. Put coffee and brandy into a heatproof bowl with the chocolate. Set the bowl over a pan of simmering water and leave until melted.
2. Remove the bowl from the heat and stir in the caster sugar, stirring until dissolved. Leave to cool.

3. Whip the cream until stiff and mix with the mascarpone and cooled chocolate mixture, whisking briefly to combine.
4. Divide the ratafia biscuits between 6 champagne flutes. Drizzle with orange juice and spoon the chocolate mixture on top.
5. Level the surfaces, spoon the double cream on each one and sprinkle with the chocolate shavings. Chill for several hours before serving.

RUM AND RAISIN FLAN

(Serves 6-8)

This looks and tastes great. I made this for the first time in York at least 10 years ago at yet again another family reunion. I was doing the cooking and have great memories of cooking on, and in, an aga.

Ingredients:

150ml/ $\frac{1}{4}$ pint double cream
225g/8oz raisins
175ml/6fl oz boiling water
85g/3oz caster sugar
$1\frac{1}{2}$ level tbsp cornflour
$\frac{1}{4}$ level tsp salt
rind and juice of $\frac{1}{2}$ lemon
rind and juice of $\frac{1}{2}$ orange
50g/2oz chopped walnuts
50g/2oz green grapes, halved and stones removed
85g/3oz butter
175g/6oz Digestive biscuits, crumbed
1 tbsp rum or rum essence
1 tsp demerara sugar

Method:

1. Place the raisins in a saucepan and cover with the boiling water. Simmer gently for about 5 minutes.
2. Mix the sugar with the cornflour and salt, stir this into the raisin mixture. Bring to the boil then add fruit juice and continue to cook until thick, stirring.
3. Remove the pan from the heat and add the orange and lemon rind then leave aside to cool, before stirring in the chopped walnuts and grapes.
4. Melt the butter, stir in the Digestive biscuit crumbs. Press into the base and sides of a an oval flan dish.
5. Spread the raisin mixture over the crumb crust.
6. Whip the cream with rum until thick then pipe round the edge of the raisin mixture and scatter with the demerara sugar.

OLD FASHIONED LEMON MERINGUE PIE

(Serves 6-8)

Homemade everything but you can cut corners and buy shortcrust pastry. Making the real lemon filling is a must.

Ingredients:

Shortcrust pastry:
165g/6oz plain flour
110g/4oz margarine
1 tbsp water

Filling and meringue topping:
55g/2oz cornflour
225g/8oz caster sugar
300ml/10fl oz/ ½ pint water
2 lemons, rind and juice
2 eggs, separated
single or double cream to serve

Method:

1. First make your pastry, by placing flour, margarine and water in a bowl and using a fork mix everything together until well combined.
2. Turn out onto a floured surface, roll out and line a metal loose bottomed flan tin 20cm/8 inches.
3. Bake blind by covering the pastry with foil or greaseproof paper and dried peas or beans to give weight and bake in a hot oven 200°C, Gas Mark 6 for about 15 minutes. Remove the paper for last five minutes to dry the pastry.
4. Meanwhile make the filling by combining cornflour, 110g/4 oz caster sugar, water and lemon rind in a saucepan and slowly bring to boil stirring until it starts to thicken. Cook for a few minutes.
5. Remove from heat and add lemon juice and egg yolks, mix well to combine.
6. Pour onto pastry case.
7. Whisk egg whites in a clean bowl until stiff then whisk in half the remaining sugar and fold in the rest of the sugar.
8. Cover the filling with egg whites making sure you have no filling showing.
9. Bake in oven 150°C, Gas Mark 2 for 25-30 minutes until meringue is golden brown and firm to touch.
10. Serve with chilled cream.

HOMEMADE ICE CREAM

Homemade ice cream, how good does that sound! - This is a basic recipe for the sort of ice cream that takes no extra beating but tastes gorgeous and is in the freezer waiting for the unexpected guests. I found the recipe years ago in a magazine and go through phases when I make it often, especially in the summer. Try your favourite liqueur poured over the vanilla ice cream.

Ingredients:

3 eggs, separated
300ml/10fl oz double cream
175g/6oz caster sugar

Method:

1 You will need a 2 litre plastic container with lid.
2. Start by beating the egg whites in a bowl until stiff, preferably using an electric mixer.
3. Gradually add the caster sugar a little at a time to make a stiff shiny mixture.
4. Whisk the cream until it just holds its shape.
5. Stir in egg yolks.
6. Now add your chosen flavour (see below) and fold everything together gently until well combined.
7. Pour into plastic container and freeze until ready to use.
8. You will find it scoops easily straight from freezer.

For flavoured ice cream, add one of the following options, I recommend them all.

- Vanilla ice cream - 2 tsp vanilla extract
- Honeycomb ice cream - 3 Crunchie bars, bashed and 3 tbsp clear honey
- Lemon meringue ice cream- 2 tbsp lemon curd (recipe in book one) and 110g/4oz broken meringue shells

CHOCOLATE SAUCE

Homemade is definitely the best and so easy.

Recipe 1

Ingredients:
225g/8oz plain chocolate
150-200ml/5-7fl oz water
55g/2oz sugar
1 tbsp clear honey

Method:
1. Warm all the ingredients over a low heat for 5-8 minutes. Stir frequently until smooth.
2. Use to pour over ice cream or profiteroles (recipe in book 1).

Recipe 2

Ingredients:
2 tsp cornflour
150ml/5 fl oz/ ¼ pint milk
25g/1oz good dark chocolate (6 squares)
3 tbsp double cream
a little sugar

Method:
1. Blend cornflour with a little of the milk in a mug.
2. Melt the chocolate in the rest of the milk and sugar to taste in a small pan.
3. Stirring, add the cornflour mixture and continue to stir, gradually add the cream.
4. Serve as above.

SWISS TOFFEE APPLE

(Serves 6)
Another old family favourite from the cream book in the 70s.

Ingredients:

150ml/ ¼ pint double cream
150ml/ ¼ pint single cream
900g/2 lbs cooking apples
135g/5oz sugar
55g/2oz butter
1 rounded tbsp golden syrup
110g/4oz cornflakes

Method:

1. Peel, core and slice apples into a saucepan, add 110g/4oz sugar and 2 tbsp of water. Cook the apples over a medium heat until soft.
2. Strain off juice from apples then liquidise fruit or press through a sieve to make a purée adding some of the strained juice if necessary to make a thick sauce. Spread sauce in a serving dish and leave aside until cold.
3. Whip the creams together until softly stiff, then spread over the apple.
4. Melt the butter and golden syrup together add the remaining 25g/1oz sugar and the cornflakes. Stir quickly together until the flakes are coated then scatter them evenly over the cream. Chill before serving.

FAMILY CHOCOLATE MOUSSE

(Serves 4-5)
This is a childhood favourite. My Godmother in Ireland knew my sister and I loved it so she made it often when we visited. As a surprise there was usually Maltesers hidden in the bottom of the dish!

Ingredients:

410g tin evaporated milk - chilled for 24 hours as this doubles the volume
2 tbsp caster sugar
2 tbsp drinking chocolate
2 tsp Camp coffee essence
4 tsp gelatine dissolved in ¼ cup cold water
1 tbsp sherry, optional
1 pack Maltesers

Method:

1. Sprinkle the gelatine in ¼ cup cold water. Leave for a few minutes to get spongey.
2. Place cup in small saucepan of water and simmer allowing the gelatine to dissolve. Cool.
3. Meanwhile beat all the other ingredients together adding the cooled gelatine at the end.
4. Pour into a glass serving dish and plop the Maltesers in one at a time. Chill.
5. Eat straight from the fridge.

Note: Don't be frightened to use gelatine. You won't go wrong if you follow instructions. Remember always add the gelatine to cold water and leave to soak, don't stir it in.

CHOCOLATE DIPPED STRAWBERRIES

These are lovely served on the side with dessert. For effect bring them to the table on a gold or silver charger plate or a pretty, wide dish.

Ingredients:

2 x 200g/9oz bars Lindt milk chocolate, melted
large strawberries with nice green stalks

Method:

1. Dip the strawberries into the chocolate holding them by the stalk. Use a teaspoon to cover them with chocolate.
2. Lay them on parchment sheets to set.
3. Use a flat knife to help lift them off the paper when set.

WHITE CHOCOLATE AND ORANGE PARFAIT

(Serves 8)
I had this at Glynda's home in Dumfries. She is an imaginative and fabulous cook. I prefer it made in ramekins or individual moulds and I make an orangey syrup and serve with orange segments. Dinner party material which is made ahead and frozen.

Ingredients:

2 oranges, one zested, both segmented
450g/1lb white chocolate
300ml/10fl oz/ ½ pint double cream
2 tsp Grand Marnier or other similar orange liqueur
300ml/10fl oz/ ½ pint full fat Greek yogurt

Method:

1. Either line a loose bottomed 20cm/8 inch round cake tin with silicon paper or as I do, line the base of individual moulds or ramekins.
2. Break chocolate into pieces and place in large bowl with half the cream.
3. Place bowl over simmering water and leave for 20-30 minutes until chocolate has melted. DO NOT STIR. Check the water does not all evaporate.
4. Meanwhile zest one of the oranges and place the zest and liqueur into a small bowl. Set aside to soak.
5. Whip cream until it just starts to hold its shape.
6. Remove the bowl of melted chocolate from the pan and beat in the yogurt. Fold in the cream and liqueur mixture.
7. Pour into the prepared tin or dishes. Cool and cover with clingfilm and freeze overnight or up to a month.
8. Take out of freezer and turn out for 30 minutes before serving if in tin or 10 minutes if individual dishes.
9. Turn out and decorate with orange segments and syrup.

To serve:
I make a syrup by boiling some granulated sugar and water in a pan and reducing. I then add a little orange juice and liqueur. Cool and add orange segments.

MARSHMALLOW CHOC POTS

(Serves 6-8)

I made this frequently years ago but lost the recipe. However I had made it so often, I can just about remember it.

Ingredients:

175g/6oz marshmallows (about 1 packet with five taken out)
135g/5oz good dark chocolate, broken up
2 eggs, separated
1 tbsp water
300mls/10fl oz/ ½ pint double cream, softly whipped

To serve:
a little sieved cocoa powder
single cream, chilled

Method:

1. Melt chocolate, marshmallows and water together in a large bowl over a pan of simmering water.
2. Add egg yolks and mix well until the mixture is smooth and glossy. Cool.
3. Beat egg whites until softly stiff and fold into chocolate mixture.
4. Finally, fold in softly whipped cream.
5. Divide between wine glasses, or individual dishes.
6. Decorate with a little sieved cocoa over the top and serve with chilled single cream.

GINGERNUT AND SHERRY LOG

(Serves 6)

A popular and easy pud. This comes from another 'Linda' who is a work colleague. We worked together in the old Elsie Inglis Maternity Hospital and share the same passion for natural childbirth and food. This log will keep for 24 hours in the fridge.

Ingredients:

300ml/10fl oz/ ½ pint Double Cream
300ml/10fl oz/ ½ pint Whipping cream
1 packet ginger snaps
1 tin mandarin orange segments
sherry, sweet or dry
plain chocolate

Method:

1. Mix creams and whip together until stiff consistency.
2. Put sherry in a bowl and soak individual biscuits for 30-45 seconds (get them out before they fall apart).
3. Sandwich together with a 1cm/ ½ inch thick layer of cream forming a long log.
4. Cover log with remaining cream.
5. Place orange segments along top of the log.
6. Grate chocolate over log to decorate.
7. Place in fridge for 1-2 hours, then enjoy.

HELEN'S RASPBERRY AND VODKA TRIFLE

(Serves 6-8)

This is a fun one, especially when you tell your guests there is vodka in it. Helen in Jedburgh is a great follower of MUMs recipes and I am delighted to have her recipe in this book.

Ingredients:

2 punnets of raspberries (fresh or frozen)
2 tbsp Vodka
2 tbsp icing sugar
1 lemon, juice and grated rind
220g/7oz white chocolate
150g pot long life ready made custard
500g carton fresh ready made custard
2 bought jam swiss rolls, sliced
150ml/5fl oz/¼pint whipping cream
grated white choc or white Maltesers to decorate

Method:

1. In a pan, heat 1 punnet of raspberries with the Vodka, icing sugar, lemon juice and rind.
2. Put it through a sieve when cool. Discard the seeds and save the juices.
3. Melt the chocolate and add to the 500g carton of fresh ready made custard which has been warmed.
4. Layer up the trifle with the slices of swiss roll, juices, the other punnet of fresh raspberries and custard in that order.
5. To finish pour the little pot of custard over and top with whipped cream then sprinkle with grated white chocolate or white Maltesers.

LEMON POTS

(Serves 4-6)

Easy, and luscious. Serve in small shot glasses or coffee cups.

Ingredients:

300ml/10fl oz/ ½pint double cream
75g/2¾oz caster sugar
juice of 1-2 lemons
thin shortbread type biscuits

Method:

1. Gently heat the cream and sugar in a pan, stirring to dissolve the sugar. Bring to the boil and bubble for 3 minutes stirring all the time.
2. Remove pan from the heat and pour in the juice of 1 lemon stirring thoroughly. It should thicken immediately. Taste, add more juice if required, it should be sweet, tangy and creamy.
3. Cool for 5 minutes, pour into small shot or sherry glasses. Cover with clingfilm, chill at least 3 hours.
4. Take out of the fridge 5-10 minutes before required. Serve with thin shortbread type biscuits.

MERINGUE BOMB AND PEPPERMINT BOMB

(Serves 6)
With either brandy and raspberry coulis or Mint Aero and Crème de Mênthe, a great dessert for a special occasion and it is frozen so is made ahead. Don't know where I got the recipe from but both these variations have been in my head for years.

Meringue Bomb

Ingredients:

300ml/ ½pint double cream
110g/4oz meringues, crushed
2 tbsp Brandy
225g/8oz raspberries
55g/2oz icing sugar, sieved

Method

1. Lightly oil a 1.2 litre/2 pint pudding dish.
2. Whip the cream with the brandy until softly stiff and stir in the broken meringues. Fold them evenly into the cream then spoon this mixture into the pudding dish. Cover with clingfilm and freeze.
3. To make the sauce press the raspberries through a sieve and sweeten to taste with sieved icing sugar.
4. To serve: turn the frozen meringue dessert out of the dish onto serving plate and defrost in fridge for about half an hour to an hour before serving so it is only lightly frozen. Serve with the sauce poured over the top and remaining sauce in a jug on the table.

Peppermint Bomb

Ingredients:

300ml/ ½pint double cream
110g/4oz meringues, crushed
25g/1oz caster sugar
1 bar of green Aero chocolate
Crème de Mênthe to serve

Method:

5. Lightly oil a 1.2 litre/2 pint pudding dish.
6 Whip the cream with the brandy until softly stiff and stir in the broken meringues and chopped chocolate. Fold them evenly into the cream then spoon this mixture into the pudding dish. Cover with clingfilm and freeze.
7. To serve: turn the frozen meringue dessert out of the dish and leave for about an hour before serving so it is only lightly frozen. Serve with Crème de Mênthe poured over.

BAKING

BROWN SODA BREAD

This is Sheila's recipe. Friends are always impressed with homemade bread and the Irish in me can't see past soda bread. My Great Grandmother had a housekeeper called Mrs Madden who made soda bread all the time. My sister and I hardly ever saw her out of the kitchen, certainly never sitting talking sociably, it just wasn't done in those days.

Ingredients:

560g/1$^{1}/_{4}$lb wheatmeal/stoneground brown flour or similar.
110g/4oz plain flour
pinch salt
2 level tsp bicarbonate of soda
2 tsp sugar
1 level tsp cream of tartar
approx 600ml/1 pint buttermilk
a little milk

Method:

1. Mix all dry ingredients together in a large bowl. Gradually mix in the buttermilk with a knife to make a stiff dough then use your hands to bring it all together.
2. Place on a floured surface and shape into a round about 20cm/8 inches in diameter. Put the loaf onto a floured baking tray and cut a deep cross in the top of the dough.
3. Place in preheated oven 180°C, Gas Mark 6 for 30-35 minutes until it is slightly risen and sounds hollow when tapped on the base.
4. Either cool on a wire tray or, as my Mum does, wrap it in a clean tea towel.
5. This can be frozen, easy to do in the quarters.

BANANA LOAF

Most people love a moist cake which uses up old bananas.

Ingredients:

225g/8oz self raising flour
2 eggs, beaten
85g/3oz butter
175g/6oz caster sugar
$^{1}/_{4}$tsp bicarbonate of soda
$^{1}/_{2}$tsp salt
450g/1lb bananas, mashed
110g/4oz walnuts, chopped

Method:

1. Preheat oven to 180°C, Gas Mark 4.
2. Mix together flour, bicarbonate of soda and salt.
3. Cream butter and sugar and add eggs a little at a time. Alternate with flour.
4. Stir in flour, bananas and walnuts.
5. Pour into loaf tin and bake for 1$^{1}/_{4}$hours.

LEMON LOAF

This is in by special request from Sally. After the carrot cake in book one this is her next favourite.

Ingredients:
110g/4oz margarine
200g/7oz caster sugar
2 eggs
rind of 1 lemon
200g/7oz self raising flour
salt
½ cup milk

Method:
1. Preheat oven to 180°C, Gas Mark 4.
2. Cream margarine and sugar.
3. Beat eggs, add rind and flour and milk alternately.
4. Pour into a loaf tin.
5. Bake for about 50 minutes.
6. Mix juice of lemon with 3 tsp of sugar.
7. Drizzle over cake when warm.

HOMEMADE OATCAKES

(Makes about 36)
What a treat, worth making your own and so easy. Lovely to serve with cheese or pâte.

Ingredients:
225g/8oz self raising flour
1 level tsp bicarbonate of soda
450g/1lb pinhead oatmeal, medium
1 tsp salt
150g/5½oz margarine or butter
90ml/3½ fl oz water
2 tbsp milk

Method:
1. Preheat oven to 180°C, Gas Mark 4.
2. Mix together dry ingredients in bowl and rub in margarine until mixture resembles breadcrumbs.
3. Stir in water and milk combination.
4. Sift some flour on work surface and roll out dough thinly. Cut into circles of 5cm/2 inches in diameter and lift onto a baking tray.
5. Bake until golden brown for 15-20 minutes.
6. Cool on wire tray until cold. Store in airtight container.

ALMOND SLICE

(Makes 12 good slices)

My Mum loves this one and makes it for her church ladies' lunch. Chrissie gave me the recipe years ago.

Ingredients:

1 pkt ready to roll shortcrust pastry
110g/4oz caster sugar
110g/4oz icing sugar
55g/2oz semolina
110g/4oz ground almonds
2 egg whites and 1 egg yolk
almond essence
apricot jam

Method:

1. Preheat oven to 190°C-200°C, Gas Mark 5-6.
2. Roll out pastry to fit a tray bake tin.
3. Mix the sugars, semolina and ground almonds together.
4. Add the eggs, essence and jam and mix together.
5. Spread mixture over pastry and cover with blanched, flaked almonds.
6. Bake for 20 minutes.
7. Cool and cut into 12 slices.

MIA'S CHOCOLATE CAKE

This is a yummy cake, especially if served warm. You can make it, clear up and eat it within one hour. I had this cake on our visit to Malawi and it holds lovely memories for me. Iain and I were invited for afternoon tea to Kim's garden. Kim helps out in the administration of the hospital. Her daughter Mia, aged 12, had made this cake and after a day in Bottom Hospital the cake was like a piece of heaven! Just for interest, in the garden were two little antelopes called Duikers but the local name is Guapi. It is the smallest Antelope in Southern Africa standing only 18 inches at the shoulder. Mrs Guapi, as she is known to Kim's family, is so tame, she comes every morning and stamps her little hooves if her cornflakes are not ready and waiting.

Ingredients:

150g/5½ oz softened butter
160g/5¾oz caster sugar
3 tbsp maple syrup
3 eggs
100g/3½oz plain flour
1 tsp baking powder
30g/1¼oz cocoa powder
a little milk
a little icing sugar for the top

Method:

1. Cream butter, sugar and maple syrup in a bowl.
2. Beat eggs in a separate mug.
3. Sift flour, baking powder and cocoa together.
4. Now gradually add the eggs a little at a time to the creamed mixture and finally beat in dry ingredients with a little milk.
5. Put the mixture into a 20cm/ 8 inch loose bottomed tin lined with silicon paper and place in preheated oven 180°C, Gas Mark 4 for 30-40 minutes.
6. Cool on baking tray. Dust with a little sieved icing sugar and serve warm or cold as preferred.

QUEEN MUM'S FAVOURITE CAKE

This recipe is old and was The Queen Mother's favourite cake. She only allowed it to be passed on to raise money for a charity. The recipe came from a lady in Jedburgh and is very like sticky toffee pudding.

Ingredients:

1 cup boiling water
225g/8oz chopped dates
1 tsp bicarbonate of soda
225g/8oz castor sugar
225g/8oz butter or margarine
55g/2oz chopped walnuts
1 egg, beaten
1 tsp baking powder
300g/10oz plain flour
pinch salt
a drop of vanilla essence

Topping:
5 tbsp light or dark soft brown sugar
2 tbsp butter
2 tbsp cream
extra chopped walnuts - optional

Method:

1. Cover the dates with boiling water and add the bicarbonate of soda. Leave to soak.
2. Meanwhile cream together the butter or margarine with the castor sugar.
3. Add in the remaining ingredients with the date mixture, mix well.
4. Bake in a 23cm x 30cm/9 x 12 inch tin in a moderate oven, 180°C, Gas Mark 4 for 50 minutes.
5. For the topping, melt the sugar, butter and cream in a pan and boil for 3 minutes only, stirring all the time.
6. Spread over the cake and sprinkle some chopped walnuts on top.

MICROWAVE CHOCOLATE CAKE

You would never believe this was made in the microwave - it is amazing. Worth using the correct baking dish because you will make this more than once. This works well with milk and margarine but for an extra rich cake use butter and cream. The cake tastes lovely with pouring double cream. I first had this at a family wedding when it was the wedding cake. My microwave is 750 watt.

Ingredients:

110g/4oz golden syrup
150g/6oz self-raising flour
110g/4oz soft dark brown sugar
55g/2oz cocoa
110g/4oz butter or margarine
1 egg, beaten
150ml/5fl oz/ ¼ pint single cream or milk

Topping:
110g/4oz margarine or butter
25g/1oz cocoa
225g/8oz icing sugar

Method:

1. Cut a strip of greaseproof paper to line the base and sides of a 23cm/9 inch pyrex or microwavable dish, deep sides needed because it rises.
2. Place syrup, brown sugar and butter or margarine in a large ovenproof bowl and microwave on high for about 2 minutes or until melted.
3. Add sieved flour and cocoa and mix well.
4. Beat in egg and then stir in the milk or cream.
5. Pour the mixture into the prepared dish and cook for 5 minutes on high (or until cooked in the centre when tested). Rotate the dish every two minutes if there is no turntable.
6. Leave to stand for 5 minutes before turning out to cool.
7. When completely cold, make the icing by mixing all the topping ingredients together

ROLO SLICE

This has got to be the most 'moreish' tray bake I have ever tasted. I can't stop eating it! Best kept in the fridge. Very easy to make.

Ingredients:

225g/8oz margarine
300g/10½oz milk chocolate (ordinary cooking chocolate will do) plus
300g/10½oz milk chocolate for the top
6 tbsp golden syrup
450g/1 lb Rolos, left whole
450g/1 lb Digestive biscuits, crumbed

Method:

1. Melt the butter, 300g/10½oz chocolate and syrup in a heavy pan.
2. Add the biscuits and Rolos. Press into a tray bake tin or small roasting tin, depending on how deep you wish it. Chill.

3. Melt the other 300g/10½oz milk chocolate, again ordinary cooking chocolate does well. Spread evenly over the top.
4. Chill and slice into pieces, not too big.

SNOWBALLS
(Makes about 30)
I had one of these last Christmas at a church fellowship meeting and had fun making them at home and eating them, so did everyone else.

Ingredients:
200g bag marshmallows
2 dessertspoons drinking chocolate
½ tin (approx 200g) condensed milk
55g/2oz butter
225g/8oz crushed Digestive biscuits
1 dessertspoon syrup

Method:
1. Melt butter, drinking chocolate, syrup and condensed milk in a pan.
2. Add crushed biscuits.
3. Wet the palm of your hand and flatten a small amount of the mixture and wrap around the marshmallow.
4. Roll in the coconut and allow to set.

CUSTARD CREAMS
(Makes 12)
Or Yo Yos as I call them because that is what they look like. The mixture only makes 12 but that just makes them all the more precious.

Ingredients:
175g/6oz plain flour
175g/6oz margarine
55g/2oz icing sugar
55g/2oz custard powder

Icing:
55g/2oz icing sugar
25g/1oz margarine
2 drops vanilla essence

Method:
1. Preheat oven to 180°C, Gas Mark 4.
2. Cream margarine and sugar.
3. Add custard powder and flour.
4. Make into a sausage shape and cut into 24. Roll into balls, lightly squash with a fork and place on a lightly greased baking tray.
5. Bake for 15 minutes.
6. Make butter icing by beating all ingredients together and use to sandwich the biscuits together.

MOIRA'S MILLIONAIRES SLICE

The best millionaires shortbread yet to taste. I am not even scared to make the toffee filling, and I have had some disasters in the past!

Ingredients:
450g/1lb butter
300g/10½oz Digestive biscuits, crushed
225g/8 oz caster sugar
4 tbsp syrup
397g tin condensed milk
250g/9oz milk chocolate

Method:
1. Melt 225g/8oz butter and make base by adding crushed Digestive biscuits to melted butter and mixing well. Press into a square, lined tin.
2. Melt 225g/8oz butter, the sugar, syrup and condensed milk. Simmer for approx 5 minutes, stirring all the time.
3. Pour over the biscuit base.
4. Cover with the melted milk chocolate.

PEPPERMINT SLICES

This was a special request for Alan my next door neighbour. The recipe was given to me by Moira who bakes a lot more than I do and always with success.

Ingredients:
225g/8oz butter
2 tbsp syrup
1 tbsp sugar
2 tbsp drinking chocolate
300g/10½oz Rich Tea biscuits, crushed
450g/1lb icing sugar
approx. 2 tbsp water
1½tbsp peppermint flavouring
1 tbsp green colouring
200g/7oz good dark chocolate

Method:
1. Melt the butter, syrup, sugar and drinking chocolate in a pan.
2. Add the crushed biscuits and put into a lined and greased square tin.
3. For the filling add the water, flavouring and colouring to the icing sugar and mix. Pour and spread over the biscuit base.
4. Top with the melted chocolate.
5. Cut into slices.

DINNER IS SERVED

I have frequently been asked for menus and suggestions for meals and entertaining and have chosen these three menus to cover three different occasions. Having used these particular menus frequently and with great success I find they are easily adapted to suit the occasion and own personal taste.

Remember these are only my ideas and you can obviously mix and match from other recipes in the book.

Menu 1 - Baked Ham Sunday Dinner

Smoked salmon pâté with melba toast (page 14)

◆

Baked ham served with celery sauce (page 33 and 56)
Creamed turnip (page 56)
Glazed carrots (page 56)
Roast potatoes (page 51)

◆

Raspberry and vodka trifle (page 67)

Menu 2 - Cold Buffet for 15

These main course recipes are from the Woman and Home magazine who kindly gave me permission to print them. I used the recommended selection and it worked beautifully! There is a lovely mixture of flavours here and it can all be prepared ahead, which is always 'my saving grace'. I have also used the menu for 6-8 people with leftovers for the next day.

Coronation chicken (page 50)
Smoked haddock tart (page 28)
Asian rice salad (page 48)
Rocket, baby gem and avocado salad (page 49)

◆

Fresh fruit pavlova (book 1 page 47)
Fudge cheesecake (page 58)

Menu 3 - Dinner party for 6

Haggis pancakes with fruity chutney and salad leaves (book 1, page 18)

◆

Chicken breast stuffed with Boursin cheese (page 38)
Wild rice with toasted cashew nuts and courgettes (page 39)
Roasted red peppers (page 39)

◆

Cappuccino choc pots (page 60)

Birth of a baby

Out of the darkness
a sunbeam of light.

Scrunched up, bunched up
opening out to display
a pink softness, a bright eye,
a delight.

A busy, frantic unfolding
wondrous life.

Written by Edinburgh community midwife **Mary O'Brien**
following a home confinement in November 2006

INDEX

SALADS & VEGETABLES 47

DESSERTS 57